# The Stranger in the Wings

*Other books by Richard Holloway:*

*Another Country, Another King* (Collins 1991)

*Who Needs Feminism?* (SPCK 1991)

*Anger, Sex, Doubt & Death* (SPCK 1992)

# The Stranger in the Wings

*Affirming Faith in a God of Surprises*

Richard Holloway

First published in Great Britain 1994
Society for Promoting Christian Knowledge
Holy Trinity Church
Marylebone Road
London NW1 4DU

British Library Cataloguing-in-Publication Data
A catalogue record for this book is available from the British Library

ISBN 0-281-04741-3

Typeset by Pioneer Associates Ltd. Perthshire

Printed in Great Britain by
BPCC Paperbacks Ltd
Member of BPCC Ltd

*For David Hutt*

# Acknowledgements

From Poem 95 by Kathleen Raine in *On a Deserted Shore* (Dolmen Press 1974), reproduced with kind permission of the author.

André Schwarz-Bart, *The Last of the Just* (Penguin 1960), reproduced with permission of Secker & Warburg (British and Commonwealth rights) and Atheneum (US rights).

From the essay 'Winston Churchill' in *Personal Impressions* © 1949, 1964 by Isaiah Berlin, with kind permission of the author, Chatto & Windus Ltd, and Viking Penguin, a division of Penguin Books USA Inc.

From E. R. Dodds (ed.) *The Collected Poems of Louis MacNeice* (Faber and Faber Ltd 1979), with kind permission of the publisher.

Translation of Boethius by Helen Waddell, from *Mediaeval Latin Lyrics* (Constable Publishers 1975), reproduced with kind permission of the publisher.

Scripture quotations are from the New Revised Standard Version of the Bible, copyright 1989 by the Division of Christian Education of the National Council of the Churches of Christ in the USA. Used by permission. All rights reserved.

# Contents

'The stranger in the wings is waiting for his cue
The fuse is always laid to some annunciation.'

*Louis MacNeice*

# Preface

The future has always been a problem for Christians. Some become obsessed with the return of Christ and what is called the apocalyptic element in Scripture in both Testaments can feed this obsession. The apocalypticist is convinced that holy Scripture contains a code that can be used to read the signs of history in order to predict the time of Christ's return or the end of the world. We know that delusionary obsessions like this are impervious to fact and reason. Even the abundantly attested fact that people have been wrongly predicting the end of all things for centuries does not budge them. 'Previous futurists got their calculations wrong, that's all, but we have the right programme now', they might say. This extraordinary phenomenon is amusingly parodied in one of the routines in 'Beyond the Fringe'. A group is led by its prophet to the top of a mountain to witness the end of all things. At the precise moment of the predicted end they start chanting, 'Now is the end'. Nothing happens. Silence descends. 'OK, same time next week', says the leader, as they struggle down the mountain.

We can expect more of this insane behaviour as we get closer to the millennium. Millenarians are unaffected by facts and repeated disappointments. Presumably, they have their reasons, their unadmitted needs, and the games they play fit their needs. The whole thing would be

innocent enough, even entertaining, if it did not sometimes fall into the hands of charismatic monsters who can
control and destroy the lives of their gullible followers.

At the other extreme is the person who has little interest in the future at all. For some reason Britain is full of
people who have a profound suspicion of the new, the surprising, the thing that is happening for the first time. Part
of this obstinacy is an entirely appropriate caution about
the dangers of 'change for its own sake', as they invariably
remind us. However, another part of it, I have come to
believe, reveals a profoundly fearful and faithless attitude
to life itself and to God, who accompanies us through it.

Much fear of the new, especially in the life of the
Christian churches, is due to what I have come to think of
as an idolatrizing of the past. This is an inescapable
human tendency, but Christians are particularly prone to
it because we are committed to an understanding of history
that sees a particular epoch as having unique significance.
The life of Jesus, the early Church and the written memories they produced have a normative importance for
Christians. It is possible, of course, to allow this normative content to guide us through time by emboldening us
to take chances in the secure knowledge that we are cher-
ished by God who calls us to live adventurously. It is just
as possible, however, and far more likely, that we will
allow the normative core of the historic faith to trap us in
a time capsule. We can persuade ourselves that the divine
action is over, that the Holy Spirit, contrary to John, chapter 16, verse 13, has no more to tell us and that the life of
faith, essentially, is a matter of remembering what God
has done and never ever a matter of discerning what God
is now doing. Discerning what God is doing is likely to be
an untidy, incomplete, and contentious activity, which is

presumably why most people do not embark upon it. It seems to me, however, that this is the kind of life to which Christian faith calls us. This book attempts to examine some of the issues, dangers, and consequences of understanding faith in this dynamic way. Increasingly, over the years, I have become persuaded that Christianity should see itself as a new and developing way of faith and not as an old and static one. 'We are the early Christians', Michael Ramsay used to proclaim with great glee.

One major consequence of this approach to Christianity is that we must give ourselves permission to take risks. One of the anxieties that bedevils the debate over the ordination of women, for instance, is the fear some people have that it might not be the will of God, and how can they find out infallibly? For many of them this will only be when the Pope tells them it is all right, but this is to subvert truth to authority. We know why people submit to it, of course. Freedom is a colossal burden, but surely this is essentially what Christianity is about. Jesus strikes me as more of a subverter and liberator than an authoritarian who fears the dangers of freedom.

In this book I wrestle with some of the difficulties of being obedient to a God of surprises, to a God who still comes as well as to a God who came. How, though, does God come? Where do we hear God's new word? In Part I, I try, in a fairly personal way, to explore these issues theologically; in Part II, I give examples of some of the practical consequences of following this theological approach. If God speaks to us from our own history, then we can expect to encounter God in the challenges of our day, among the homeless, among people with AIDS, in the lives of those who try to care for others and of those engaged in political struggle. Each chapter in Part II has an independent history, but is the result of my recent pre-occupation with the themes rehearsed in Part I.

I have added a personal, rather sorrowful afterword. It seems to me that one of the most tragic aspects of contemporary Church history is the failure of the Anglo-Catholic movement to deal creatively with the issues raised by this book. At the time of writing it is hard to tell what the future will hold, but it is entirely likely that Anglo-Catholicism, as we have known it, will vanish from the mainstream of Anglican life in the next generation, either by large-scale defections to Rome or by some mechanism of internal disaffiliation within the Anglican Church that will isolate it and cause it to wither in the bitterness of exile. This was an outcome I predicted in 1978. I was invited to be one of the keynote speakers at the first Catholic Renewal Conference at Loughborough in 1978. The address was applauded, but it was clearly not heard. In 1989, in a mood of sorrowful anger, I wrote an essay I called 'Tract 1990'. It was a call to Anglo-Catholics to leave the *Titanic* in which they were cruising to oblivion and start a new initiative that would free them to address the issues of the future, not fight the battles of the past. That process has already started. I pray that this book will help it on its way.

Finally, on a different note, I am extremely grateful to my secretary, Christine Roy, for her labours in typing various drafts of this book and for her cheerful and efficient support.

Richard Holloway
*Edinburgh*
1993

# Part I

A fascinating question, of course, is which came first: the institutional realities of human history or our image of the divine reality? Which way does the projection operate? Did the human project the divine, or was it the other way round? Is our imaging of God simply a magnified and majestic projection of human experience, or are authoritarian models of human relationships genuine reflections of the divine order? Some analysis of a favourite Victorian hymn will throw an interesting light on this question. You will not find the verse in any modern hymnbook that I have come across, but when Mrs Alexander wrote that all-time favourite, 'All things bright and beautiful', she included a verse that exactly reflected the image of God and society that I have been outlining:

> The rich man in his castle,
> The poor man at his gate,
> God made them, high or lowly,
> And ordered their estate.

The next time you use that hymn at a children's service or at your local school you will not sing that verse. We have dropped it because, presumably, it no longer reflects our theory of society.

Yet what has happened to the theory of God that lay behind that particular theory of society? If we can drop one, why can we not drop the other? If we no longer believe that God orders human society into ascending steps of privilege, then why did we *ever* believe it? If we no longer believe that hierarchical and authoritarian societies reflect the mind or will of the God who orders our estate, then what happens to our image of God as almighty, as in control, as God of power and might? If fixed authoritarian social structures are no longer held to reflect the divine reality, is it not perhaps worth contemplating the possibility that the traditional fixed authoritarian picture of God was itself a reflection of human experience and not the other way round?

The intriguing thing about all this is that it is the New Testament itself that is most subversive of the image of God that has stood at the back of much Western theology. If we look briefly at three great texts from the New Testament, we discover that the God made known in Christ, what John Taylor would call the 'Christ-like God', is completely different to the official definitions of God that have prevailed for centuries. According to Philippians chapter 2, the God made known in Christ is not a controlling authoritarian reality, but a self-emptying being whose generosity leads it to assume the form of the slave, not the form of the ruler. Further, in Mark's Gospel chapter 10, in the famous Zebedee encounter, Jesus goes out of his way to say quite explicitly to his apostles that the way the world orders things, in hierarchies, power structures, and models of control, is precisely *not* the nature of God. He advises the apostles not to let these seductive worldly models invade the way they order their lives: 'It shall not be so among you', he tells them. Littleness, not greatness, is to be the Christian paradigm; service, not authority and control. We see the character of such a God disclosed in Matthew chapter 5 in the beatitudes, the great reversals, where everything desirable or sought after and fought over in worldly experience is reversed and called blessed: poverty, grief, meekness, justice, mercy, persecutions and revilings are the estates blessed by God.

So, who *is* God? How can we talk of God, imagine God? We are not going to follow it, but the wisest course would be to remain silent and to remember Maggie Ross's statement that God cannot be conceived, God can only be encountered. Nevertheless, we are creatures who use language and sometimes only know that we know something when we have put it into words. We are, therefore, destined to struggle with language and concepts, to find the words that approximate to the realities we encounter. We must recognize a fundamental difficulty with this at the outset: language can sometimes suggest the reality of the thing to which it refers, but it can never *be* the thing to which it refers. This is true when we are talking about one another and human experience; it is trebly true in our attempts to describe spiritual realities. Language is analogical, it describes by likening one thing to another; or it is metaphorical, it operates by using dramatic figures of speech that suggest the reality of the thing described in an image or a sound sequence, such as Tennyson's

> The moan of doves in immemorial elms,
> And murmuring of innumerable bees.[1]

Language is revelatory. It can bring us close to the reality described but we always have to remember that it is not itself the reality. It is an interpretation, a way of thinking about something, but never exactly the thing in itself; it is flesh made word. So the first thing we must recognize is that all talk, including God-talk, is approximate; it expresses the reality on which it gazes in figure and in code. In order to reach some way towards encounter with the thing described, the reality beyond the figures of speech, we have to engage in an interpretative activity. We have to sit under the language and let it suggest realities to us, but must not be tyrannized by the language itself. This is particularly true when we talk of divine things. Only God is God. Theology is God-talk, not God-self. If we were truly faithful and secure creatures we would find this liberating, but in our insecurity and uncertainty we find it frightening. We constantly fall into the same trap, the trap that the children of Israel fell into in the wilderness. They were not content with the elusive reality of the invisible, intangible God Moses revealed to them, so they ordered Aaron to make them a God they could really get their mind round, could really get in touch with, a portable god, an idol. This idolatrizing dynamic is still powerfully active in the human imagination. Idolatry, not atheism, is the biggest enemy of the true God. Idolatry is to make something that is relative and contingent into something absolute and undiscardable, so that it becomes as God for us. Anything can be an idol—an aesthetic tradition, including a particular prayer book, a text of Scripture, a liturgical practice, an architectural arrangement, a fixed method of relating the genders to each other, all of these and many other things can be made into fixed immutable realities—idols. Anything can become an idol. The interesting thing to note about an idol is that it is usually something that has at some time genuinely mediated something of the divine. It becomes an idol when we cling to it long past its 'sell by' date. The thing that once conveyed something of the divine to us becomes a substitute for the divine, something we would rather have than God, because it has become important to us for its own sake, not because it was a vehicle that once conveyed significance to us. However, only God is God; everything else is relative. If it is God we seek, and not an idol to command and comfort us, then we must constantly be abandoning places and systems through which God once spoke in order to keep up with God, who will not be trapped or entombed in any system or category.

How, then, do we talk of God? With great lightness and

reserve, remembering some of the issues that we have already explored. Our first major reservation has to be that the relationship between God and the historic context of human culture is a two-way street. Our idea of God will obviously, if we are genuinely committed to it, influence our human systems, but it is beyond debate that our human systems themselves reflect and influence the way we image God.

A tiny digression into theological history will illustrate this point. According to the classic definition of God, God is impassible. God, according to the Thirty-Nine Articles, has neither body, parts nor passion. God is impassible. Impassibility, from which comes the more useful word impassive, suggests remoteness, detachment and distance—categories that exactly express the character of the ruler in authoritarian societies and absolute monarchies. We are back where we started, asking which came first? Surely, though, there can be little doubt now that our theories of God reflect cultural conditions, so it is theologically fatal to fix our description of God for all time, because human categories shift and lose their usefulness as indicators of the divine reality. So committed was the Church to the notion that God could not suffer, the impassibility of God, that Patripassianism, the conviction that God could suffer, was categorized as a heresy in the early Church. God the Son suffered in the flesh of Jesus Christ, but God the Father was impassible and could not suffer. It has been an unsympathetic doctrine to many down the ages. Abelard among others can be interpreted as opposing it in the Middle Ages, but it is in our own day that it has been overthrown as an adequate way of expressing our experience of the nature of God. One of the strongest Patripassians in English Church history was Woodbine

Willie, Studdart Kennedy, the famous First World War chaplain, who saw mystically that God was not detached from the slaughter in the trenches, but was down there in the mud being put to a perpetual shame. Of course, in our own era, a distinguished theologian like Jurgen Moltmann can write an acclaimed book entitled *The Crucified God* (translated by R. A. Wilson and J. Bowden, SCM 1976). This little episode in theological history shows how language about God is relative in its usefulness to us, in that it depends on the way in which it accords and resonates with our own human experience.

Our problem in most religious circles today is that the originating matrix for most of the religious language we use is a particular social system called patriarchy. Patriarchy was the way things were organized for centuries and the word itself need not be used in an entirely negative sense. There are suggestions of strength, protection and order in the image projected by patriarchal societies. On the other hand, and to be brutally specific, if you have ever counselled a woman who has been sexually abused by her father you will find it a very limiting and problematic way of defining God. Patriarchies are highly articulated social structures in which the father is at the top of the pyramid. They can, of course, be communities of love rather than arrangements for the arbitrary expression of power, but any system that concentrates power is intrinisically abusive. Patriarchal structures for centuries, however unknowingly, have oppressed women. Our difficulty, and it is a genuine difficulty, is that we have inherited this understanding of the divine reality, this way of talking about God. It has formed us in our conscious and unconscious parts and it is very difficult for us to get it out of our minds, to achieve a shift of consciousness, to discover a new paradigm, a new way of expressing the eternal reality of God, whom we seek and long for.

We have already seen that another metaphor for God, associated with the patriarchal one, is to describe God as 'almighty'. For centuries we have begun our prayers almost unthinkingly with the phrase 'Almighty God'. It is a phrase that gathers up our memories of apparently settled and ordered days, when God was in heaven and all was well with the world. Even so, the term 'almighty' is itself problematic. It clearly does not and cannot mean that God can do anything. Can God make two plus two equal seven, for instance? No, we would say. It means that God is true to God's own nature. Nevertheless, the word 'almighty' has to be identified as a military metaphor, as a probable translation of *Yahweh Sabaoth*, the Lord God of Hosts, the God of the armies of Israel. I suspect that for most of us this way of speaking about God is unsympathetic and does not reflect contemporary sensibilities. Neither, I believe, does it reflect the self-emptying nature of God that we have already reflected upon in those subversive passages at the heart of the New Testament. Today we prefer categories that suggest the mercifulness and vulnerability of God. Speaking personally, I prefer the version of the *Sanctus* that goes, 'Holy, holy, holy, *vulnerable* God', to the military snap to attention of the contemporary *Sanctus* in modern liturgies, 'Holy, holy, holy, God of power and might'.

The challenge in using appropriate language for God is to find categories that will express our own experience of the divine nature, but which, at the same time, seek to protect the Godness of God, the otherness of God. The word 'almighty' can be seen to be, in some sense, an honorific, not a definitional description of God, rather in the way that we refer to the Queen as Your Majesty. Nevertheless, the word 'almighty' raises an ancient philosophical problem that shows the danger of pushing any description of God to extremes. The old conundrum goes, 'If God is good, he cannot be almighty. If almighty, he cannot be good'. This dilemma is irresolvable only if we treat language about God with too much reverence and give it a sort of quasi divinity in its own right. If, instead, we acknowledge that all language about God has been evolved in response not only to genuine experiences of the divine, but to human realities as well, then we are able to interpret it historically, contextually, and see it as something fluid, varied, even discardable. More important still, we can see it as something living and evolving, something that expresses the permanent human struggle with the divine, so we should expect the human encounter with God to be generating new metaphors, new languages, new forms of God-talk. Our contemporary preoccupations will themselves one day seem as finite and relative as the things that preoccupied our forebears, but that will be up to the generations that lie ahead of ours. Today, it is our responsibility to find categories that express our experience without turning them into idols, rigid and fixed.

As a matter of fact, we prefer language about God today that emphasizes the self-limiting, self-emptying nature of God, the God who accompanies us in our sorrows, who goes with us to Calvary, Auschwitz and Srebenica; the God who is the victim of all human arrogance, tyranny and power, the crucified God, still journeying to Jerusalem on bandaged feet to die for us. Some of us are increasingly finding meaning and solace in imaging God as feminine, as mother and lover, as sister. Some of us have come to believe that centuries of male dominance, both of the Church and theology, have rendered us incapable of entering a whole dimension of God that half the human race can help us to experience. If humanity is made in the image of God, male and female, then we can, in some legitimate sense, argue back analogically from the human to the divine reality, and the human reality is female as well as male. Today we are giving ourselves permission to acknowledge the feminine in God and to discover new depths of encounter with the divine as a result.

We must not, of course, fall into the ancient human trap of fundamentalizing our own experience and the language that best describes our contemporary encounter with the divine. Only God is God and our language can never exhaust the reality of the divine nature. Nevertheless, we should have confidence in our own experience of God and trust it as the way God is being mediated to us today. It seems to me that the best approach to God-language is an inclusive and incremental one in which we open our arms as widely as we can and embrace as many categories of language and experience as we can, remembering F. D. Maurice's epigram, that 'we are usually right in what we affirm and wrong in what we deny'.

I think I can best sum up what I have been trying to say by recounting an experience I had at Taizé some years ago. I was invited to visit Taizé, near Lyons, France, by Brother Roger, the Prior and Founder of the order, and I prepared for my first encounter with the community there with great excitement. The thing I was most looking forward to was taking part in the Taizé office. I had used the Taizé office book for a number of years in the early 1970s and remembered its richness and diversity. In creating their form of prayer, the brothers had borrowed from the

great monastic traditions and had, I thought, achieved a
remarkable work of liturgical art. The Taizé office book
followed the Christian year with a suitably embroidered
richness of expression. I looked forward to sitting in the
chapel at Taizé and listening to the white-cowled brothers
singing their elaborate office in impeccable Gelineau
chants. It was in this mood that I went to evening prayer
on my first day at Taizé. The place was packed with young
people from all over the world. I noticed that the brothers
had had one of the walls of the great church they had built
for the community knocked out and had added a tent-
like structure on to it, to accommodate more people. The
office itself was not what I expected. I was deeply moved
by it, but I was intrigued by its simplicity: some chants,
a few verses of Scripture read in six or seven different
languages, a psalm, and a long period of silence. At supper
with the brothers after the evening office, I asked them
about their form of prayer. What had happened to the
Taizé office book? 'Ah, yes,' they said, 'we still have it, of
course. Indeed, we are proud of it. But God started sending
all these young people to us from all over the world and it
was quite obvious that the form of prayer we had developed for ourselves was not appropriate to these new circumstances, so we abandoned it. Everything is provisional,
you know. Only God is God.'

The power of the provisional, the doctrine of provisionality, is a profoundly important and liberating one that
rescues us from all the idolatries, which are the greatest
enemy of God. Scripture is full of images that make the
same point. They describe the life of faith as a journey
through a wilderness and believers as pioneers, not people
settled in  permanent communities with houses built on
fixed foundations. God is always up ahead of us, leading

us on through history, inviting us to discover the divine through our own contemporary experience and not to lock God on to the past. I think this is a particular danger for the Church of England, which has inherited so many wonderful old buildings and a marvellous old liturgy. It is difficult to resist the notion that God's most significant activity has been somewhere back in the past and that it is the duty of the Church to preserve what God has *done* rather than identify what God is *doing*. This understanding of the Church sees it as the spiritual arm of the National Trust, part of the heritage industry, there to preserve and conserve what has been, never ever to be concerned with what may be coming to pass. This whole nostalgic theory of Christianity traps us in the past and makes us idolaters. The doctrine of provisionality, if we will let it, will rescue us from these idolatrizing superstitions.

We are only human, though. We are fearful and not very imaginative. We can expect to find ourselves clinging, like Mary Magdalene, to the modalities of the past. Most of us are clinging in guilt to our own failures and sins, refusing to accept the God who wipes out our sinful past and calls us, new-born, into another day. We will find ourselves clinging to ideas, institutions, structures, even words that no longer mediate the living God, because they have become substitutes for God and not provisional means through which God touches our lives and hearts. All this is painful to acknowledge and even more painful to do something about, because it calls us to live by faith, to go out without security, without possessions, having given everything away in order that we might find the pearl of great price, God, who calls us to participate in the divine life. It means that we are called to a life of turbulence and discomfort, a travelling life, a life that does not tie us down too long to any one place. Our own longing for permanence screams against this institutional home-lessness. We want the settled life, the life of the graveyard where little happens, but where we can water the flowers and gaze at the gravestones and remember the past with affection. But our God is a grave-buster, a tombstone roller, a wandering God, calling us to leave the graveyard and follow him into Galilee. To be Christians we have to resign ourselves to an exciting life. Unamuno captured it perfectly: 'May God deny you peace but give you glory'.[2]

# 2

# *The Stranger in the Wings*

Walkerburn is a name that evokes fond memories for generations of Scottish Episcopalians. Walkerburn is a small mill town in the Tweed Valley. It sits above the Tweed, beneath a spur of the Moorfoot Hills. On the hillside of the little town are two large mansions, built for wealthy mill owners, that were given to the Society of Saint Peter, a women's religious order. For most of this century the community maintained the houses as a retreat centre for the Scottish Church. The sisters and a few permanent guests lived in the house called Sunnybrae, while those on retreat stayed at Stoneyhill a little further up the hill. Above the houses swept a magnificent hill called Priesthope, and the bedrooms in Stoneyhill commanded a view of the Tweed Valley and Minchmuir Hill beyond. Generations of Scottish priests spent their preordination retreats there, and went back time after time to be quiet by themselves or to lead their parishioners on retreat. I spent my deacon's retreat there in September 1959, and I can remember being challenged to race another ordinand up Priesthope Hill. We arrived back for compline soaking wet and aching all over. I spent my priest's retreat there the following June, and I returned at least once a year for the next eighteen years.

It was an old-fashioned retreat house—guests were expected to do nothing except make their own beds. They accommodated about twenty people on retreat. We prayed at Stoneyhill, where there was a lovely chapel through which the afternoon sun filtered, but we dined down the hill at Sunnybrae. The dining-room had a single long table, covered with a freshly laundered tablecloth, and those on retreat had their own linen napkins. Everything was served by the sisters. By the time I was ordained, they were all very old, but no tradition was altered—there was no self-service at Sunnybrae! Every dish was brought slowly and sometimes precariously from the kitchen by the elderly sisters, their cassocks gently slapping round their ankles as they served their guests.

By 1975, it became obvious that the community could not continue to run the place for much longer. The Society of Saint Peter was attracting no new vocations and the remaining sisters were too old and tired to continue to run the retreat house. Sadly, they prepared to leave Scotland and return to their mother house in England. They tried to find another community to continue their work, but without success. The houses were sold and reverted to their original use as private dwellings, and all the furnishings were given away. It was a mournful passing for us all, but especially for the sisters who saw their life's work being dismantled before their eyes. The whole episode induced in me a mood of elegy and regret for the dear dead past, perfectly summed up in a few lines from Kathleen Raine:

> If I could turn
> Upon my finger the bright ring of time
> The now of then
> I would bring back again.[1]

This longing for 'the now of then' seems to be an innate human characteristic; we constantly look back to the way we were. The paradox of memory is that when we actually lived the now of then it did not seem so special, but seen through the tinted lens of nostalgia it is fixed forever in a golden glow. This elegiac mood is one of the tricks of remembrance. Human beings are remembrancers. We have seen only the past and as, like doubting Thomas, we tend to believe only what we have seen, we can end up believing only in yesterday.

Before they finally left Walkerburn, the sisters had a farewell party and I went to it. It was a tearful affair, almost a wake, but I found on their noticeboard a quotation that pulled me out of my mood of nostalgic self-absorption. It was a few lines of poetry sent to the sisters by a member of an enclosed order in England. I took a copy of it at the time and have often meditated on it:

> Look back, remember, and have confidence;
> The future, like the past, has God in it;
> His cupped hands bear the whole of time, and you;
> The future holds nothing that can elude
> His covenanted care and mastery.[2]

Those lines reminded me that Christians are called to believe in what they have not yet seen. They are called to believe that God is God of the future as well as the past, but to discover the God of the future they sometimes have to learn to let go of the God of the past. This kind of painful letting go is a human experience before we encounter it in our relationship with God. Our own human history teaches us its truth before we turn to divine history.

It is, for instance, a lesson that wise parents learn. We are perhaps happiest as parents during the childhood of our children—those years of wonder and trust, when our hearts sometimes seem almost to burst with love for them.

The temptation that faces all parents is to cling to their children long after they should have released them into their own future. We discover that when we let them go from us as children, we get them back as adult friends.

The same difficult lesson is learned in bereavement. I have known people who have never recovered from the death of a loved one. I remember one parishioner who left her husband's chair exactly the way it was the night he died in it. On the table by the chair lay the half-smoked pipe he had put down just before the heart attack. The book he was reading was still there, marked where he had left it. This had all happened years ago, but in her shock and sorrow she had never been able to let go of the memory of that night. Her whole life had become a mourning, her whole energy dedicated to keeping the shrine of her husband's memory. We know now that grief is a slow and complicated process, that we cannot speed it up, we cannot microwave our own psycho-spiritual evolution, but we also know that, to move into the future, the bereaved must, at some stage, let go of the past, and own and acknowledge the death of the one they have lost.

The same is true in the field of ideas. They say that there is nothing more powerful than an idea whose time has come; but it is also true that there is nothing sadder than clinging to an idea whose time has gone, whether it is a failed ideal, a false theory or a concept that has lost its usefulness. Holding on to it stops us discovering the new thing that might reignite our passion and commitment. To discover the meaning of the risen Christ, the Christ of the future, Mary Magdalene had to let go of the Jesus of the past.

This tug of war between the past and the future has characterized humanity's relationship with God from the beginning. God comes to us from our future, but we are tempted to dwell on where God has been in our past. The Israelites did it in the wilderness: they looked back with nostalgia to the days of their captivity in Egypt. We find the same note of elegy and regret in the resurrection narratives. 'Why look for the living among the dead?' we read in Luke. 'He is not back there, He is risen', Matthew reminds us. Think, too, of the mood of plangent regret in the conversation of the two who trudged to Emmaus: 'We had hoped that he was the one to redeem Israel' (Luke 24.21).

We find the same mood in the post-resurrection community, when they were coming to terms with the meaning of the resurrection. One strong impulse in the young community was to turn the memory of Jesus into a cult, to develop a kind of Elvis theology, that would freeze the memory of Jesus and sanctify everything associated with him. There is even a hint that the more conservative of our Lord's followers, particularly his brother James, wanted to confine the cult to Jerusalem. Jesus would live there in their memories. This is where he had been crucified. It was good for them to stay there, caught up forever in those glorious memories, but the Holy Spirit was not having that and provoked the first of many disputes in the Christian community. The fifteenth chapter of the Acts of the Apostles is a delicately edited account of that dispute. It guaranteed the universal mission of the Church and the opening of the faith to the gentiles, though compromises were made with the conservatives in Jerusalem, to whom concessions were offered in the form of submission to a moderated observance of the Jewish ritual code, excluding circumcision but including some of the dietary laws. Versions of that episode have been rerun throughout

Christian history. God wants to give us new things, but we cannot receive them because our hands are clasped too tightly round the old.

From the beginning there has been a tension between the risen Christ who comes from the future and his followers who are constantly visiting his graveside. There has been a struggle between the freedom of Christ and the immobilizing insecurity of his followers. Yet Christ told us to look forward to the new things he had prepared for us. This is one of the great themes in John's Gospel, which is made quite explicit in chapter 16, verses 12 and 13:

> I have yet many things to say to you, but you cannot bear them now. When the spirit of truth comes, he will guide you into all the truth; for he will not speak on his own authority, but whatever he hears he will speak, and he will declare to you the things that are to come.

From the beginning a developmental energy has been intrinsic to the Christian movement. Christianity is a way of discovery, a conviction that God comes to us not only from the past and its memories, but from the future, from the very collisions of history itself.

How, though, are we to hear God's new ideas, discover the new things God has prepared for us? How can we identify them, where do they come from? Let us turn to Scripture and use it dynamically, reading it in a way that will disclose the mind of God for us now. The first portion of Scripture I would like to look at is from Matthew chapter 15, verses 21–28:

> Jesus left that place and went away to the district of Tyre and Sidon. Just then a Canaanite women from that region came out and started shouting, 'Have mercy on me, Lord, Son of David; my daughter is tormented

by a demon'. But he did not answer her at all. And his
disciples came and urged him, saying, 'Send her away,
for she keeps shouting after us'. He answered, 'I was
sent only to the lost sheep of the house of Israel'. But
she came and knelt before him, saying, 'Lord, help me'.
He answered, 'It is not fair to take the children's food
and throw it to the dogs'. She said, 'Yes, Lord, yet even
the dogs eat the crumbs that fall from their master's
tables'. Then Jesus answered her, 'Woman, great is your
faith! Let it be done for you as you wish'. And her
daughter was healed instantly.

It is notoriously difficult to enter our Lord's consciousness
through the stories in Scripture. I used to interpret this
unattractive encounter in a way that put Jesus in a more
flattering light than a bare reading of the narrative allows.
Without hearing his tone of voice, it is difficult to capture
the mind of our Lord. On the face of it, Jesus, intent only
on a ministry to the children of Israel, is challenged by a
pagan woman, a gentile, to heal her daughter and he
ignores her plea. His silence does not tell us much. Was it
a contemptuous, a racist silence? Was it the silence of
uncertainty or was our Lord playing a game with her? That
is what I used to think. This narrative, I thought, was evidence of our Lord's gift for irony. Calling her a dog and
refusing her the bread that belonged to the children of
Israel was a joke that she caught and threw back at him.
Now I am not so sure. I think this woman changed our
Lord's mind about something fundamental, was the
means whereby he made a new discovery.

There are three elements in the story. The first is the
woman's need, through which God speaks a new word to
Jesus. The second element is the resistance the new idea
provokes. The apostles tell Jesus to send her away because

she is shouting after them. Their ideas about God's way with the world were complete, closed and impenetrable; they already knew God's will, nothing new was needed, nothing fresh could enter. The third element in the event is our Lord himself. Formed as he was by the traditions of his people and deep in his reverence for them, he is also radically committed to the will of God as a present reality, so he is able to hear God say a new thing through this woman from the margins, this woman on the periphery of his consciousness. He hears her and responds to her request and a new thing happens. The first step in the universalizing of the gospel is taken. The Church universal is here today because a new thing was heard and responded to then.

We find a related event in our second piece of Scripture, from the Acts of the Apostles, chapter 10, verses 9–16, though the whole chapter should be read:

> About noon the next day, as they were on their journey and approaching the city, Peter went up on the roof to pray. He became hungry and wanted something to eat; and while it was being prepared, he fell into a trance. He saw the heaven opened and something like a large sheet coming down, being lowered to the ground by its four corners. In it were all kinds of four-footed creatures and reptiles and birds of the air. Then he heard a voice saying, 'Get up, Peter; kill and eat'. But Peter said, 'By no means, Lord: for I have never eaten anything that is profane or unclean'. The voice said to him again, a second time, 'What God has made clean, you must not call profane'. This happened three times, and the thing was suddenly taken up to heaven.

The background to the chapter is the great Judaic

controversy in the early Church, to which we have already alluded. Was Christianity a sect within Judaism, built round a particular cult of Jesus of Nazareth, or was it a universal message that was to be taken to the ends of the earth? The debate, like all Church disputes, had its conservatives, its compromisers and its radicals. James, the Lord's brother, was the conservative. Paul, the upstart, was the radical. Peter was the compromiser, the very model of an Anglican bishop caught uncomfortably in the crossfire. In chapter 10 of Acts, two stories are going on at the same time, expertly woven together. The precipitating factors are the spiritual yearning of Cornelius and Peter's anxiety about the great dispute that is tearing the young Church apart.

In the previous story we saw God using an outsider to speak a new word to our Lord. The same tactic is used here: God speaks to Peter through a dream. Today we would probably say that Peter's unconscious doubts were clamouring for attention and forced themselves into his mind in the dream. God speaks a new word to Peter in the dream, but he resists it. His theological system is complete and impenetrable; nothing new can enter it. We must notice a particular irony here. We know that the voice Peter hears is the voice of God telling him to kill and eat these unclean creatures, but Peter quotes God back at God. He reminds God that he is the author of the very code he is inviting Peter to abrogate. We could meditate long on this mysterious ambiguity, but it does seem to suggest not that God changes his mind, but that things that were once appropriate to our spiritual development may one day no longer be appropriate and we must learn to abandon them. Though Peter resisted, part of him was open to God and was genuinely struggling with the issues that confronted him. Finally he listened to the word, and in his subsequent encounter with Cornelius he acts upon the new insight and Cornelius and his household are baptized. It does not end there, of course. We know that Peter, having made the decision intellectually, had a bit of emotional catching up to do. He continued to slither round the issue for a number of years, much to the disgust of Paul, who had the radical's contempt for the sloppy anxieties of the liberal intellect.

In both of these passages we watch the struggle with a new idea; they show us something of the dynamics of revelation. There is the insider for whom everything is sewn up and there is the outsider on the margin, looking in, calling for entry. Note that God speaks to the insider through the agency of the person on the edge, on the margins. The first reaction is resistance to the notion that we should listen at all to these strident people on the edge of things: 'Send them away, they come shouting after us', is our first, uncomfortable reaction. If there is any openness at all to the work of the Spirit, however, any chink in our armour through which God's disturbing word can penetrate, then a new word is heard, a change is made and we move on to the next uncomfortable challenge. This is the pattern of holy Scripture, but it is also the pattern of the 'scripture' of our own lives. We must learn to read the 'scripture' of our own lives, using the written Scripture as the key of interpretation.

In my own experience, I have found that this three-fold pattern of challenge, resistance and acceptance has defined many of the moments in my own moral, spiritual and theological development. Let me intrude a personal memory that illustrates my thesis. When I moved to the United States in 1980, I was contemptuous of the growing interest in inclusive language in both the Church and society. It seemed to me that the old system worked pretty well, people knew where they were with it, and that exclusive language, gender-specific usage, was a convenient way in which to handle complicated issues. I made jokes about the infelicities of the politically correct vocabulary that was emerging.* Fortunately, in the parish in which I worked there were many highly intelligent Christian women who refused, in their regard for me, to let me get away with my unexamined attitudes. Gradually, through their advocacy, I began to hear what they were saying and to feel something of the pain they felt when the Church's linguistic usage appeared to discount their own presence and integrity. Finally, my resistance was eroded and I heard a new word from God. Now I am persuaded that the Church must be increasingly sensitive in these matters, not only to the language of worship, but to the very categories and metaphors of theology. Only God is God; everything else, including our language about God, is provisional and expendable. To cling to a particular usage is a form of idolatry, and can be a species of cruelty. It is the same three-fold pattern: hearing a voice from the margins, the periphery of one's own concerns, initial resistance, gradual acceptance of the new word and then moving on. The sources of these revelations, these new words God is saying to us, seem to be areas that we prefer to overlook or ignore. The people who present the most painful challenge to the Church are the people on the margins of society, the victims and casualties of our social structures.

* It is, in fact, the inelegance of much politically correct vocabulary that is its worst enemy. The worst one I have come across recently is from a version of the Resurrection story: 'Go and tell the apostles that the child of person has risen from among the ontologically challenged.'

If Scripture is to be believed, God not only speaks to us from this perimeter of tragedy that surrounds our comfort, but is to be found dwelling there.

One of the things that Archbishop Oscar Romero discovered in El Salvador was that he had no gospel for the poor, but that they had a gospel for him. He struggled to find a message for the poor, when all the time God was trying to say something to him through them. Finally, they evangelized him. He heard God speak through them, he responded and gave his life for the gospel. There are other examples of the same paradoxical evangelism.

It is one of the supreme ironies of our culture, for example, that the AIDS community, which has been dismissed by certain hard-edged Christian groups as sinners who are being punished by God for their wickedness, has shown itself to many of us as a paradigm of the gospel itself. If the gospel is about the unconditional love and Grace of God meeting human extremity in its need, then the response within the gay community to the challenge of HIV is a very paradigm of the gospel itself. God is fond of these ironies, of course, and delights in confounding the wise in their wisdom and the mighty in their strength by preaching the foolishness of the cross. If we would encounter a new word from God, we must step out of our safe enclosures and encounter God on the edge.

This dynamic of divine encounter is something that is true of our own spiritual development. Many of us spend years ignoring our own private outsider—the part of our nature we refuse to acknowledge or deal with, the disturbing, strident voice, say, of our own sexuality, or the doubting, questioning truth-seeking child within us that we dare not listen to because it might overturn the conventions that upholster our lives. These are voices we must listen to and acknowledge if we are to grow spiritually, because, almost certainly, God will be speaking a new word to us through them. Then there is holy Scripture itself, which many of us are tempted to treat in a proprietorial way, as if we already know all about it and what it means. When we submit to its voice in deep prayer and openness of mind, we can find it alarmingly new and brutally challenging. The fourth source of these discomfiting revelations will be our own critics, the people who are least likely to collude with our own picture of ourselves. They come to us the way Nathan came to King David, 'Thou art the one'—they challenge us. If we can hear and receive their word, new things happen.

If there is truth in this exposition of the God who teaches us new things through the ministry of the marginalized, there are several very severe consequences for all of us—personal, historical and theological. It must be quite obvious that our own history will affect what we hear and the way we hear, so when a new challenge comes, we have to interrogate ourselves. What are the interests, the forces, the factors of resistance that are likely to inhibit our hearing of the new word? Radical self-knowledge is a fundamental principal of spiritual evolution. Plato said that the unexamined life was not worth living. Those who have read the novel or seen the film, *Howard's End*, will get the point. The key phrase is, 'Only connect'. It is about a group of people who fail to connect their own experiences of personal failure to the reality of other people's lives. The novel, in many ways, is a commentary on the Lord's Prayer, 'forgive us our sins as we forgive those who sin against us'. Connecting with God and with others can only be done on the basis of an honest self-knowledge.

The second consequence of the fact that God comes to

us from the future, from the edges of things, concerns our understanding of history. We must have a doctrine of God as active in history, so that we are prepared to discern the divine challenge for our own time. This dynamic of continuing revelation is likely to be encountered in the great movements of the human spirit, the great upheavals of history. Let me mention two areas where the divine challenge is being placed before us today. The first is the environmental crisis, which challenges us to a new theory of our relationship with the creation and a new discipline and responsibility towards it. Because of the fashionable nature of the concern, some of us are likely to be resistant to it, but it is a theme that illustrates the three-fold law of revelation, whereby we are challenged from the edge, offer initial resistance, then hear and own the reality of the situation and respond with action. The second great area of challenge that confronts us is the emergence of a new global politics that transcends nationalism and offers us a vision of human unity and interdependence. It is, of course, no accident that at the very moment when this vision is laid before us there should be a resurgence of crude nationalism, sometimes of the brutal Bosnian variety, sometimes of the nostalgic English sort. Each is characterized by a profound fear of the new and a refusal to acknowledge that it could come with blessings in its hand.

History sometimes produces politicians of genius who help us to embrace the future. Franklin D. Roosevelt was such a man. It is worth meditating on something written about him by Isaiah Berlin:

Roosevelt stands out principally by his astonishing appetite for life and for his apparently complete freedom from fear of the future; as a man who welcomed the future as such, and conveyed the feeling that whatever the times might bring, all would be grist to his mill, nothing would be too formidable or crushing to be subdued and used and moulded into the pattern of the new and unpredictable form of life, into the building of which he, Roosevelt, and his allies and devoted subordinates would throw themselves with unheard of energy and gusto. This avid anticipation of the future, the lack of nervous fear that the wave might prove too big or violent to navigate, contrasts most sharply with the uneasy longing to insulate themselves so clear in Stalin or Chamberlain.

So passionate a faith in the future, so untroubled a confidence in one's power to mould it, when it is allied to a capacity for realistic appraisal of its true contours, implies an exceptionally sensitive awareness, conscious or half conscious, of the tendencies of one's milieu, of the desires, hopes, fears, loves, hatreds, of the human beings who compose it, of what are impersonally described as social and individual 'trends'. Roosevelt had this sensibility developed to the point of genius. He acquired the symbolic significance that he retained throughout his presidency, largely because he sensed the tendencies of his time and their projections into the future to a most uncommon degree. His sense, not only of the movement of American public opinion but of the general direction in which the larger human society of his time was moving, was what is called uncanny. The inner currents, the tremors and complicated convolutions of this movement, seemed to register themselves within his nervous system with a kind of seismographical accuracy. The majority of his fellow citizens recognized this—some with enthusiasm, others with gloom or bitter indignation. Peoples far beyond the frontiers of the United States rightly looked to him as the most genuine and unswerving spokesman of democracy of his time, the most contemporary, the most outward-looking, the boldest, the most imaginative, the most large-spirited, free from the obsessions of an inner life, with an unparalleled capacity for creating confidence in the power of his insight, his foresight, and his capacity genuinely to identify himself with the ideals of humble people.

The feeling of being at home not merely in the present but in the future, of knowing where he was going and by what means and why, made him, until his health was finally undermined, buoyant and gay; made him delight in the company of the most varied and opposed individuals, provided that they embodied some specific aspect of the turbulent stream of life, stood actively for the forward movement in their particular world, whatever it might be. And this inner *élan* made up, and more than made up, for faults of intellect or character that his enemies—and his victims—never ceased to point out. He seemed genuinely unaffected by their taunts: what he could not abide was, before all, passivity, stillness, melancholy, fear of life or preoccupation with eternity or death, however great the insight or delicate the sensibility by which they were accompanied.[3]

Rooseveltian courage and confidence towards the future is rare; it is the mark of the true leader and it emboldens us to confront the signs of the times.

The final consequence for us of a commitment to a God who is in the future as well as in the past lies in the area of theology. It will clearly commit us to theology as a dynamic, not static, enterprise, and to tradition as a living thing in which we ourselves are passionately engaged. Too often Christian theology has been seen as a kind of pass-the-parcel game in which we simply hand on a prepacked body of truth, whereas the reality is different. We are not handing on a sort of eternal, shrink-wrapped, impenetrable object. We are engaged in a living relationship with a God who was and is and is to come. Such a God will be surprising us with new challenges in language, in imagery, in the theology of power and leadership, in the understanding of structure and ministry in the Church, and in traditions of worship. Such a God will speak to theologians through the trends of the day, through the women's movement and encounter with other faiths, and through the overwhelming challenge of the new poverty, the new underclass that disfigures the so-called liberal democracies of the West. The one thing we will not find in following such a God is uninterrupted tranquillity.

The Christian movement is a great adventure in which we accompany the risen Lord of history in a pilgrimage through time—our own time, and time yet to come. This is a challenging vision that should embolden and exhilarate us. It is captured for me in one of Louis MacNeice's poems entitled 'Mutations':

> For every static world that you or I impose
> Upon the real one must crack at times, and new
> Patterns from new disorders open like a rose,
> And old assumptions yield to new sensation;
> The stranger in the wings is waiting for his cue
> The fuse is always laid to some annunciation.[4]

That is almost as exciting a challenge as the resurrection narratives, where the messengers at the graveside tell the bemused apostles that 'he is not here, he is risen' and goes before them into Galilee. Galilee is the future. We are to follow him there.

# 3

## Auto-ecclesiology

When I was twelve, a little cousin who lived up the street from us died of meningitis. This was in 1946, the year after the Second World War ended. Her father, my namesake, was still abroad with the Navy. We lived near the school I attended and it was normal for me to come home in the middle of the day for lunch. That morning, however, my mother told me to come to my cousin's house, up the street, where she would be, comforting the bereaved mother. While I was there, eating my soup, the Rector from the local church came in to arrange the funeral. He asked who I was and commanded me to appear at church on Sunday to enrol as a server. It is hard to get inside my own mind as it was then, to relive the now of then, but I do not remember any particular reluctance about obeying him, though I had never been a churchgoer before. My mother was a believer, though not until later a great churchgoer. All I could testify to was a sort of implicit agreement that there was a God to whom we were somehow related. What experience I had had of church was pretty boring, though the kids in our street frequently attended the local Ebenezer Chapel, mainly because they gave us tea and Paris buns after the lantern slide shows. I had no idea what to expect at St Mungo's. Father Mackay, the Rector, was a very advanced churchman and he had converted this middle-of-the-road church into an Anglo-Catholic shrine. On the altar there was a tabernacle, flanked by six candles. Incense was used at worship, and, after Evensong on Sundays, there was Adoration of the Blessed Sacrament.

I knew nothing about any of this when I made my way to Burnbrae, to St Mungo's, the following Sunday. When I got there, I fell in love with it all. Looking back, I can see that it was an aesthetic conversion. I was converted by beauty. I had only the haziest idea about what it all meant or what religion was about, but I was captivated by the mystery and the beauty of the liturgy. I can remember the excitement with which I learned to use the missal given to me by Father Mackay. I was particularly captivated by the woodcuts that illustrated the book, especially the woodcut for the Feast of All Saints. It showed a priest at the altar elevating the host at mass, while behind him knelt the Deacon and Subdeacon. Above the altar, with its six proud candles, there were companies of angels adoring the lamb that stood on a cloud, below a triangle representing the Trinity, directly above the elevated host. I did not have a clue about what it all meant, but it spoke of something tremendous and other-worldly and I was captivated by it. I do not know whether I was susceptible to holy places before my first visit to St Mungo's, but I have certainly been susceptible ever since. In my youthful ignorance I was captured by the sense of the holy, the otherness, the beauty of God. I did not know the lines then, but I had clearly come to one of those places that are the world's end, in Eliot's phrase. I had looked across the frontier and caught a glimpse of the beauty of God.

In my untutored way, I was experiencing the primordial element in religion, which is adoration of the sheer Godness of God, the beauty of God. In the beginning, before theology or morality or any institutionalizing of the experience, human beings are drawn to God for God's own sake; they fall in love with God. That is what had happened to me. That primary experience strikes me still as being truer, less studied, than anything else that succeeded it in my encounters with Christianity.

Eighteen months later, when I told Father Mackay that I wanted to become a priest, he arranged for me to go to the Cottage at Kelham, where they tried to train uneducated boys like me for the Anglican ministry. By this time I had been confirmed and knew a bit about how to serve in the sanctuary, but I was still ignorant about Christianity as a whole. I can distinctly remember going up to the Rectory the night before I was due to leave for Kelham, aged fourteen. I wanted some kind of comfort and reassurance, because I was already feeling homesick at the thought of leaving Scotland. I picked up a bible in Father Mackay's study, but did not know how to use it. I had a sense that I could find some comfort in it, but did not know where to look. I opened it at the beginning of the book of Genesis and read the account of the creation, from which I derived no consolation whatsoever.

At Kelham, the beauty that had drawn me towards God through Catholic liturgy was reinforced, but something else was added to it. I fell in love with monasticism, with the ideal of total abandonment to God in a community separated from the world. In particular, I fell in love with the Trappist ideal of work and silence, and I started playing at being a monk. The straightforward response of adoration to God's beauty was being overlaid with self-consciousness and a sort of pity for God. I remember this hitting me with particular fierceness one Good Friday when I walked in the grounds at Kelham after the Three Hours Devotion. I could hear lorries groaning from miles away on the great North Road and I wrote a self-dramatizing little poem lamenting the fact that, while God was being crucified, the busy world went on its indifferent way. I was beginning to experience the Church not as a window through which the beauty of God shone, but as a community of perfection in a fallen world. We had seen the vision beautiful, while others in their ignorance worshipped mere reflections, projections of that originating beauty.

Two things were happening here. The first was a kind of pitying protectiveness towards God; related to it was a sense of election, a sense that we, at least, knew the truth and were surrendering our lives to glorify it. Interestingly enough, there was still very little theology in this experience. However self-conscious the experience was becoming, God was still a reality to be enjoyed, not talked about or organized. The impulse of prayer was still the primary reaction to the reality of God. A coating of self-consciousness and self-importance was beginning to cover the innocent gladness of God worship, but the primary instinct was still there, the instinct of adoration. This was what Baron Friedrich von Hügel called the mystical element in religion, as opposed to either the intellectual or the institutional.

According to some interpretations of von Hügel's three-fold typology, it is the mystical that succeeds the other two, whereas in my experience it was the other way round. I first encountered dogmatic Christianity in West Africa. I am using 'dogmatic' in the technical sense as used by the Church to define its truth-declaring function. A dogma is a revealed truth defined by the Church. My difficulty with dogmatic theology, in this sense, is not that there are dogmas, but that there are so many dogmas, so many things, ideas, concepts, institutions for which the Church has claimed a hallowed status. In my ritualistic adolescence I had learned to prize many liturgical practices and to be contemptuous of many others, but I was not a dogmatic Christian in the sense that I had encountered an absolute belief system that allowed little latitude in interpretation. This was rectified in West Africa.

In 1956 I was sent out by Kelham to become the Secretary to the new Bishop of Accra, a Kelham father and the last white bishop in Ghana. Having been brought up in a country that had a Presbyterian ethos, I suppose I had unconsciously absorbed a relativistic approach towards the polity of Christian churches, an indifference to the way they ordered their ministerial arrangements. Not having got to that part of the course at Kelham, I was, as yet, innocent and untutored in my attitude towards the ordained ministry. It seemed self-evident to me that ministries of any sort were an organizational arrangement, a convenience, a human way of doing things. It had not previously occurred to me that they themselves could be held to be arrangements of intrinsic worth.

I remember discussing this with the Bishop of Accra one evening and discovering, to my surprise, that we had a different attitude towards his authority as a bishop. There was nothing personal in this. I must have demonstrated a rather functional understanding of the episcopate as the way, perhaps the best way, in which the Church had chosen to organize itself. Doubtless there were historical, not to say psychological reasons, for the different polities, largely presbyterian in Scotland, largely episcopalian in England. Implicitly, I suppose, I was leaning towards a doctrine of ministerial interchangeability. It had not previously occurred to me that, whatever the differences between the

presbyterian and episcopalian systems, they could be anything more than human disagreements. I suppose, even
then, I was an implicit pluralist in my attitude to religious
structures. However, I was severely corrected by the
Bishop, who pointed out to me that the order of bishops in
the Anglican Communion was not a functional convenience, not even an anciently hallowed functional
convenience, but a divinely mandated succession through
which the apostolic authority was passed on to the
Church. You were either in it or out of it; you either had
Christ's authority to function as a church or you did not
have it. In my naive way, I had believed that it was the
Church that was the divine mystery, the important reality
through which the vision of God was mediated; and that
the Church had organized itself in different ways at different times in response to different pressures. Now, though,
I was being initiated into the view that the ministry somehow validated the Church, or was at least the ground on
which the Church was built.

The doctrine puzzled me, though I could see its advantages. I could see that it was important to protect the
Church from charlatans, from self-appointed prophets or
messiahs, and that it was almost inevitable that some
method of authentication or certification would emerge in
the Church. This made obvious human sense. Standards
had to be protected, people had to be guarded against
exploitation. All of that seemed obvious and empirical to
me—common sense. What I was hearing from the Bishop,
however, was that the significance of ordination, and
especially of episcopal ordination, resided on an entirely
higher plane. It was not a human structure, a sensible way
of organizing things and getting them done efficiently; it
was a supernatural reality, through which the authority

of Christ was passed on in a quite literal sense through a human conduit of tactile succession. It followed from this theory, of course, that if you were unlucky or delinquent enough to have broken away from this chain of succession, you ceased to be part of the Church, in the orginal sense, at all.

The theory induced in me a mood of theological anxiety. If the mystery of the Church was guaranteed by a supernatural mechanism that was, in theory, traceable like an energy cable under a city street, but which was, for all practical purposes, untraceable at certain points in history, then how could we be absolutely certain that we were connected to the cable in the first place? It had ceased to be a matter of spiritual, or even doctrinal succession. It had been reduced to a blunt physicality into which you were either introduced or from which you were excluded. It necessitated a new vocabulary, where words like 'valid' and 'irregular' had currency. The consequences of invalidity are profound. Human parallels are difficult to discover. The quack doctor, for example, is not a perfect parallel. The quack is not a doctor and has no authorization or certification. If quacks are discovered impersonating doctors they are subject to the law. The distinction is there to protect the profession from impostors, as well as to protect lay people from incompetent practitioners, but, in theory, submitting unknowingly to the attentions of a quack need not imperil us. It is quite possible that the quack has certain medical or surgical skills. We might even benefit from his or her atttentions. So, a quack masquerading invalidly as a doctor may or may not endanger us, whereas an invalidly ordained minister, according to this theory of orders, will deprive us of the sacraments. The theory is quite simple. Only those ministers of the sacraments who have been ordained by people who were themselves validly ordained, and so on back to the apostles, have the power and authority to celebrate the sacraments of the Church. For instance, according to Roman Catholic teaching on the subject, I, ordained for over thirty years in the Anglican Church, have never celebrated the Eucharist, absolved a penitent or, since becoming a bishop, confirmed a lay person or ordained anyone to Holy Orders. I have gone through the motions, but nothing has 'taken'.

The whole discussion, of course, moves in an extraordinarily unspiritual realm. It is a brilliant example of the way elusive spiritual mysteries become reified by the institutions that the originating spiritual vision gave rise to. My seminar with the Bishop of Accra initiated me into a realm of theological anxiety. It pointed to a precarious state of affairs where whole groups of people could be deprived of the sacraments because they belonged to ecclesial structures that had been cut off from the power lines of apostolic succession. So, I started asking questions about where the Church was.

The two big players in this particular game were obviously the Roman Catholic and Orthodox churches. They each recognized the other as being within the apostolic succession. While neither much liked the other, and the Orthodox Church, in particular, deeply resented papal claims, nevertheless, each recognized the other as being able to produce valid, saving sacraments. The Anglican Church claimed to belong with the 'big two': it had preserved apostolic succession and, therefore, had validly ordained ministers, unlike most of the other reformed churches, which abandoned this theory of order altogether. The fact that Rome and Orthodoxy dismissed our orders as absolutely null and utterly void did little to alleviate my anxiety about the whole matter, and the branch theory of catholicity did little to help.

The branch theory, greatly loved by certain Anglicans, is the doctrine that, while Anglicanism is not itself the Catholic Church, it is a valid branch thereof, one that has grown over the wall and drooped down into the field next door. The main tree over the wall tried to pretend that it did not exist and would not look at it, but the branch knew where it came from and, while it was saddened by the rejection of the main trunk, it knew in itself that it was a real part of the tree, even though this awkward wall obscured the fact.

An even more attractive version of this teaching was caught by Evelyn Underhill in a throwaway remark. Like many Anglicans of a Catholic persuasion, she had suffered acute anxieties about the true Catholic nature of her own Church of England. She agonized long and hard about becoming a Roman Catholic, though Baron von Hügel, her spiritual adviser, told her it is usually better, in spiritual matters, to stay where you are. She finally settled the matter to her own satisfaction by declaring that, while the Anglican Church might not be the city of God, it is a respectable suburb thereof.

By the time of these revelations, I had moved a long way from the simple recognitions of my boyhood. I had moved into a complicated world in which it is hard to tell right from wrong and truth from error. Even though I felt intrinsically repelled by this mechanistic theory of order that subjected the delicacy of spiritual relationships to brutally physical realities, I went along with it for years and can remember treating members of non-episcopal churches with condescension, if not contempt. In a mysterious kind of way, I had inverted the normal order of von

Hügel's classification of religious experience into the mystical, the institutional, and the intellectual.

It is sometimes suggested that the institutional is the infant stage of spiritual development. It represents the immature need for structures and boundaries, orders and authorities. The intellectual phase, on the other hand, is a later development that is like the adolescent or young adulthood phase when we are asking questions and doubting our way to knowledge, sometimes false knowledge, sometimes feeling our way out of belief or into over-belief. The final phase, the mystical phase, according to this typology, reflects an adult balance and acceptance of mystery and elusiveness as the mature spiritual reality. No one moves through the phases successively and, indeed, we can very easily revert to previous phases as we respond to challenges and changes. It seems to me now that my initial encounter with the mystery of God, as mediated by the Church, had had a purity and innocence of enjoyment about it that was spiritually more mature than the anguish over and obsession with lines of demarcation and institutional validity that characterized the ecclesiological preoccupations of my early manhood.

A part of me always felt slightly ashamed of this position. The Christians I met from non-episcopal systems all seemed to me to be no less, if no more, spiritually healthy than those who received their sacraments from a purer source. All this time, I was visited by reminders of my earlier, more innocent self, who muttered in my ear that the whole theory was intrinsically unlikely and beside the point; more importantly, it was morally dubious, because it seemed to cast God and Christ in the role of spiritual engineers, rather than the elusive but beautiful mysteries of my original experience. My collusion with ecclesiastical fundamentalism was probably more to do with theological insecurity than anything else, but it was gradually eroded by two factors. George Bernard Shaw once said that every profession is a conspiracy against the laity. When I was ordained I began to realize that, almost inevitably, a professional ministerial caste is bound to develop protectionist structures and theologies to support them. The effect of this has been to demarcate the Church and, as official Roman Catholic Canon Law still does, identify it essentially with the clerical caste, which is the part of the Church that guarantees the validity and soundness of the rest.

A part of me has always acknowledged the need for structure and organization for reasons of human efficiency, decency, and order. Another part of me responded excitedly to the drama and solemnity of high theories of order; but the deepest part of me found it hard to believe that this was the way God had precisely ordered things. It seemed unlike the God made known in Christ, whose main passion seemed to be to remove unnecessary burdens from the shoulders of God's little ones. I was, in fact, experiencing the potent and fruitful tension between what Paul Tillich called 'the Catholic substance and the Protestant principle'. I knew myself to be increasingly Catholic, but a Reformed or Protestant Catholic: Catholic in my love for the beauty of the tradition, its use of sight, sound, colour, its celebration of the senses, of history, and of human culture; Protestant in my awareness that any or all of this could become a substitute for God instead of the means whereby spiritual realities are conveyed to us. It is the problem of idolatry all over again. The temptation is always to turn the means into an end, to make the provisional into the ultimate, the relative into the absolute, but only

God is God—everything else is provisional, including all the wonderfully hallowed mechanisms that humans have evolved to explain and convey something of the divine mystery to one another.

It was by means of the Protestant principle—by which I understand the questioning and prophetic element in spirituality, which is wary of the way all systems domesticate the wildness of God into manageable structures—that I found the necessary balance. It was this principle that provided me with a key to the other aspect of Christian history that began by baffling me, but which, in time, I came to celebrate. This was the area of conflict in ideas. Like most Christians, I was brought up to believe that the Christian norm was a kind of theological placidity or tranquillity, in which all ideas smoothly interlocked into gleaming continuities of truth. This theory seemed markedly at variance with the reality of Christian history, which showed that, from the very beginning, there has been a level of turbulence that is extreme, though it is probably outmatched by the controversies within Judaism itself, from which we came.

I found myself moving from a dogmatic model of the Church as an authoritative structure for the mediation of truth, towards a theory of the Church as the algebra of truth-seeking. Truth, I have come to realize, is not a packaged commodity, handed out by a central bank that manages the currency of ideas; it is the result of conflict and collision, and is never absolute. According to the conflict theory of truth-seeking, a truth is stated and a counter-truth is posed against it. The resulting collision of truth with truth sometimes leads to a synthesis that transcends the previous level of understanding. This process is never at an end, so the best protection for truth is freedom. It seems to me increasingly likely, therefore, that the best way to guarantee the full and paradoxical freedom of truth is within multiform structures, plural structures that allow enough space for paradox, that are quicker to affirm than to deny and are prepared to allow tares to grow among the wheat, because they are more interested in harvesting the wheat than in eradicating the weeds.

This way of doing theology creates more of an atmosphere, an ethos, than a strict structure. It is as interested in *how* we think as in *what* we think, and it seems to operate on the basis of three principles. First of all, it has a marked lack of interest in human theories that attempt to explain the mysteries of Grace. What is given it affirms, but it is not greatly interested in the supernatural physics that bring the mystery to pass. This is in contrast to some other theological traditions, such as the great metaphysical theories of Roman Catholicism or the antimetaphysical realism of the radically reformed tradition in theology. This way of looking at theology is best illustrated by the example of the Eucharist.

Most of the great controversies concerning the Eucharist are about the nature of the presence of Christ in this sacrament. Roman Catholic theology has sought to explain the nature of that presence by means of the metaphysical theory transubstantiation, while Reformation theology, partly in reaction to this type of philosophical positivism, has often appeared to explain the mystery away by reducing the Eucharist to a memorial service. Anglican theology has done neither. In our customs, such as the direction to the minister to consume what is left of the elements, and in our liturgy, especially in that classic of Anglican eucharistic devotion, The Prayer of Humble Access (for some reason greatly disliked by modern liturgists), we accept the reality of the presence, but we refuse to offer any explanation of it. Our attitude is best summed up in the words of Queen Elizabeth I:

> 'Twas God the word that spake it,
> He took the bread and brake it;
> And what the word did make it;
> That I believe, and take it.[1]

Individual Anglicans may be transubstantiationists, consubstantiationists, receptionists or memorialists privately, but there is no official commitment to any of these theories, though Article twenty-eight explicitly rejects transubstantiation. Bishop Guest, who drew up the paragraph in Article twenty-eight that denounces transubstantiation, expressly stated that it was drawn up not to 'exclude the presence of Christ's body from the Sacrament, but only the grossness and sensibleness in the receiving thereof'.

So, Anglicans practise a sort of theological modesty that affirms the mysteries of faith, without offering too much comment on how they work. We are content to let Grace be Grace, knowing that it has its own power, its own language, spoken to the soul. We resist the temptation to stick explanatory labels on everything.

A second important modifier for us, and one we have already noticed, is a recognition of the paradoxical nature of truth, its sweep and width, and the certainty that we are not equipped to see it all in its contradictory fullness. One of the fascinating things about theology is its ability to correct and balance itself historically. Individuals and generations see things from a limited perspective. The sociology of knowledge has underlined the importance of the context in which we know, and this context includes temperament and personal history as well as our attempts to be objective.

It follows, therefore, that we will almost certainly see some things that are hidden from others, but, by the same token, we will fail to see what is plain to them. There is a tendency to fundamentalize our own angle of vision and discount what others see. Theological conflict, like most philosophical conflict, is usually between opposing truths, rarely between truth and error. This insight encourages theological modesty. In actual Anglican history this modesty before the truth has led to the creation of the Anglican theological continuum. We may enthusiastically occupy a particular spot on that continuum but, as Anglicans, we must learn the difficult art of affirming the whole stretch of truth. This is not the consequence of a shallow relativism. It is the result of a passionate commitment to the nature of truth itself.

Third, and related to our understanding of truth, is our theology of history. We have a historical and, therefore, a dynamic understanding of revelation. Christian theology is controversial, because it believes in a God who is revealed in history. For us, both the present *and* the past tenses are important. Scripture is normative for us, but it is not an absolutely fixed point. It is more like a vast lake than a huge mountain. It pours through history, irrigating culture and society, changing the shape of things, never continuing in one stay. Christian theology is conservative in the sense that it is a constant dialogue with the past, but it is a dialogue, not a monologue. Out of God's treasury come things new as well as old. Scripture itself is an example of this dynamic, continuous interchange. The emergence of the canon of Scripture happened within history, it was an historical process, a process of dialogue and disagreement.

The Anglican approach is best seen in contrast. Unlike those whose sole authority is Scripture, we do not accept the static nature of revelation; unlike the Roman Catholic approach, with its creative interpretation of tradition, we refuse to engage in the production of new dogma. We have a dynamic understanding of truth, ordering it in hierarchies of importance, acknowledging areas in which we are less free to tamper, recognizing lower orders of truth with which we are more free to experiment and explore, allowing us a flexibility in response to the Holy Spirit at work in history and culture, remembering that all language about God is metaphorical and is not itself to be idolatrized. This gives us a sort of reverent courage in the way we do theology.

Given these three modifying principles—a bias towards pragmatism rather than theory, a modesty before the scope and width of truth itself, and a dynamic view of history as the continuing vehicle of God's revelation—what else can we say about the Christian ministry as we have received it? First of all, we have to admit to a period of great confusion and experimentation in the early Church, most of which is hidden from us. Out of this vortex, two things emerged: a canon of Scripture and a tradition of ministry built on an order of bishops, whose authority was delegated and diffused through an order of presbyters. Some people see this as the triumph of order over charisma, institutional dynamics over freedom of the spirit. Wandering prophets, it is claimed, were once allowed to celebrate the Eucharist, before the episcopate cornered the market. Others would claim that the Church had learned the dangers of a privatized ministry and recognized that people should not take this ministry upon themselves without the consent of the Church.

From the beginning, there has been built into the ministry a tension between charisma and authority, holiness and certification. Some traditions resolve the tension by laicizing the sacramental function, while others have banished sacraments altogether as it was felt that they created unnecessary functional divisions within the people of God. We can acknowledge the force of these solutions without repudiating the wisdom of what emerged in the Catholic tradition. What emerged was an ordering of functions within the body of the Church, with the bishop as the focus of authority. The priesthood emerged as a derived or delegated ministry, reflected today in oaths of obedience and licences to officiate. The emergence of the episcopate gives rise to interesting historical questions, most of them unanswerable. The main question takes three common forms:

- Did the apostolic ministry arise before the Church and constitute the Church?
- Did it arise with the Church, in parallel, as it were, giving rise to a sort of dual authority?
- Did it arise from the Church and is it, therefore, dependent on the Church?

The Anglican Church has accepted the traditional orders of ministry without committing itself to a water-tight theory of its origins. Article thirty-six on the consecration of bishops and ministers simply points to the ordinal and the ordinal takes it all for granted. We accepted the mystery of Christ's presence in the Eucharist without theorizing about it.

The same goes for apostolic succession. We are not quite sure if the succession matters, but we are sure we are in it and we make sure we keep it going in the way we consecrate bishops. Yet Richard Hooker, the main creator of Anglican theological method, was not rigid regarding theories of succession. In Book III of his *Of the Laws of Ecclesiastical Polity* (ed. W. S. Hill, Harvard University Press 1977), he refuted the Puritan contention that, 'in Scripture there must be of necessitie contained a forme of Church politie the lawes whereof may in no wise be altered'. This is why Anglicans ought to have little difficulty with the ordination of women. It is a matter that comes firmly within that area of the Church's organization where both variety and change are permitted. It was Hooker's contention that forms of polity were matters of discipline, not of faith, and that considerable local differences could be allowed. Even so, in Hooker, as in Anglican thought generally, there is enormous reverence for the enduring *fact* of traditional ministerial order.

If we accept the fact of traditional ministerial order, do we have to commit ourselves to the theories that have grown up around it? There is the essentialist theory I was introduced to by the Bishop of Accra, which sees ordination as imparting a new ontological character to the person ordained. That is, something more than simply institutional authorization is imparted at ordination and it can never be withdrawn. Power, as well as authority, is imparted. Authorization may be withdrawn, but the indelible mark upon the soul can never be effaced.

There is the functionalist view of ministry, which sees it as a straightforward convenience or division of labour. Things have to be taken care of, jobs have to be done, so let us stop the mystification and get on with it. This gives rise to the professionalizing of the ministry. The strength of this approach is that it can increase competence. Its weakness is that it can lead to careerism. Functionalists demythologize and deromanticize ministry, but what they gain in logic and efficiency they may lose in poetry and passion.

A third approach attempts to get out of the dilemma created by the tension between essentialist and functionalist arguments. This sees ordination as the entry into a new relationship with the Church. We join ourselves to an order at ordination, just as we enter a new and ordered relationship when we marry. There may not be the imparting of an indelible substance, but a profound change in relationship is effected and we are no longer what we were before.

These models of ordination have one thing in common: they emphasize the disciplined side of ministry. They affirm the wisdom of the tradition that has guarded ordination against individualism and theological privatization. People cannot take the ministry on themselves, nor can they simply ordain the ministers they want. There is an 'otherness' about the ministry, an apartness, that is also clearly within the Church. This safeguards the people of God against the dangers of appointing spiritual mascots or private chaplains.

Speaking personally, I have experimented with all three approaches and settled, finally, on none. As a boy, I sensed that it was what came through the Church that was important, not the Church itself. Time has brought me back to where I started, but with a sense of knowing it for the first time. The ecclesial family I stumbled into as a boy has turned out to be the one that has allowed me to experiment with and discard various theologies. It has taught me that there is some truth in most things but no monopoly of truth in any particular thing. We are constantly tempted to remove the tension and discomfort involved in truth-seeking by foreclosing the argument or by shunting ourselves into sidings of the like-minded instead of braving the realities of contention and dissent. It seems to me that the Catholic consciousness needs the probing critical analysis of the Protestant principle, if it is to avoid institutional tyranny and spiritual monopoly; while the Protestant principle requires the richness of the Catholic tradition, in all its paradox and confusion, if it is not to revert to a mean-spirited scepticism that denies more than it affirms and quenches the generous spirit.

Theologically, I travel lighter these days. My long relationship with the Church has settled into a mould of affectionate wariness. In technical language, I now see the Church as an eschatological sign that points away from itself to the reality of God and God's promise that the kingdom will come on earth, though never in its fullness. There has been a tendency in Christian history to identify the Church with the kingdom, the kingdom being the totality of the divine mystery in its encounter with the human mystery. This identification of Church and kingdom is another manifestation of idolatrizing arrogance. It is obvious to any fair-minded person that God is as active outside the Church as inside it. The Church is less than the kingdom, but it points towards it. It is an association of men and women that aims at losing itself in the kingdom, so it ought to affirm kingdom realities, divine initiatives, outside the Church. That is why people who take this approach are not intimidated when they are accused of getting their ideas from the secular sphere. This should hold no surprises for people who have ceased to identify Church and kingdom. It is this recognition that has allowed, indeed encouraged, Christians to associate and work with people in kingdom activities outside the Church, in politics, in works of mercy, in social provision, in combating the evils that disfigure human history. The Church is an association that points away from itself to the mystery of God, but it is still, for all its ambiguity, a place of encounter with the divine beauty. It is most like itself when it ceases to justify or explain itself and turns to worship the God made known in Christ. It is at its best when, in the language of the Letter to the Hebrews, it endures as seeing the one who is invisible. That is what drew me out of the back streets of the Vale of Leven when I was a boy of twelve. It is what still holds me.

# 4

## The Spiritual Supermarket

When I was a boy I used to do the weekly shopping for an old blind woman who lived across the street. Her name was Granny Watson and 'going for her messages' was simple. The Co-op was up the street and it offered little choice, so shopping presented few problems and no existential angst. I always bought a quarter-pound packet of tea for her, and there was only one kind of tea on sale. I bought half a pound of cheese, but there were only two kinds of cheese, and she always wanted white Cheddar. There were two kinds of bread offered, plain loaves and pan loaves, but in our street we ate plain. The only people who ate pan loaves in our town were the school teachers and lawyers who lived up the hill. The simplicity of shopping for food was also a parable of the religious situation. As with cheese and bread, there were really only two brands on offer: the Catholics and the Protestants. Episcopalians were the exception that proved the rule, because we were an exotic hybrid of the two dominant brands.

Shopping today is different. We have gone from the village shop to the supermarket, and shopping is no longer just a practical necessity. For many it has become a way of life, what they do with their spare time. In our new consumer culture it has become one of our favourite pastimes. Supermarkets are the new shrines. We could even adapt the old epigram and say that the family that shops

together stays together. The modern supermarket is a
place of almost infinite choice and it poses challenges
that lead to endless anxiety: which brand of coffee will I
try this week, what new cheese from this bewildering
array, and will plain Darjeeling do, or should I try something more exotic, such as this tea blended with rose
petals?

Even so, shopping is still a parable of the religious
situation. We have gone from a situation that presented
one religion in two brands, where we were either one or
the other, to a situation that offers a bewildering range of
experiences, from highbrow atheism to black magic and
everything in between. It is said that nowadays we know
the price of everything and the value of nothing, so it
becomes increasingly difficult for people to make discerning choices when there are so many spiritual commodities
shiningly packaged to attract our attention. The name
given to this modern phenomenon is 'relativism', because
that is the main characteristic of what philosophers call
'modernity' or even 'post-modernity'. The main assumption
of modernity is that everything is relative, nothing is
absolute, nothing is better than anything else. The old
simple choices are no longer before us. At least five elements have contributed to the position we find ourselves
in today and their cumulative impact has served to banish
much of the security that previously attended belief.

The first major element has been contributed by what is
called 'the sociology of knowledge', the study of what
human beings are doing when they claim to know things.
The major discovery in this area is that the context influences how we know and what we know. Of course, this is
not an absolutely new insight, but in this century it has
been applied with a rigour that has eroded much of the

confidence with which we previously claimed to know things. An illustration might help here. In an article in *The Independent*, Peter Jenkins wrote several years ago:

> Meyerhold, the great Russian theatre director, used to tell a story from his days as a law student at Moscow University. One of the professors would arrange for a powerful thug to rush into the classroom in the middle of the lecture, there would be a fight, the police would be called and the troublemaker removed. Then the students would be asked to recount what had happened. Each would tell a different tale. Some would even insist there had been not one thug but two. 'Hence', the professor would explain, 'the Russian saying "He lies like an eye witness" '.

Contexts, both internal and external, influence the way we see things and what we claim to know, and knowledge of this fact has intruded an air of hesitancy into those areas that are most difficult to verify, especially in the field of religion. Expressions like, 'point of view' and 'private opinion', reflect the way in which religion has been relegated to the private sphere. Religion is now what we call a 'soft' not a 'hard' topic, that is, it is no longer one that can be precisely defined or demonstrated by scientific proof.

The second of these five elements is a specific application of this principle of the relativity of knowledge to the field of sacred history. The main core of the Christian faith is what we call revelation. Christians have never believed that their religion was a purely human construct, but that it has developed as a response to a divine initiative, a self-showing of God, a revelation. How, though, is this revelation brought about? How does God come through? How do we sift the divine from the instruments that disclose it?

Lots of rival claims are made about revelation. Some claim, for instance, that Scripture came into being by means of a kind of automatic writing process, the ancient authors writing down precisely the words dictated to them by the Holy Spirit, so that every word comes directly from God. Others offer a more naturalistic explanation and see openness to revelation as the same kind of inspiration artists experience. Wherever art comes from, it is mediated through human instruments and they always particularize or individualize it in the process.

Another important question is this: is revelation ever specific, is it always general, or can it be both? Does God intrude himself through specific events and specific people, or is God's influence general and more abstract? Musings like this have placed a great question mark over the whole meaning of divine revelation and the history of the critical study of Scripture in the last 150 years has made the status of the Bible confusing for many people. In the Victorian era the crisis was mainly about the Old Testament. In our era the battle is being fought over the New Testament. It is a complicated and subtle debate and the effect of it is to undermine the confidence that many people feel about the status of Scripture. If it is not straight scientific history, what is it? How are we to understand it? We only have to notice the squeals of outrage that usually follow Bishop Jenkins' public musings on the subject to see how involved and painful an issue it has become. What seems to be at stake is the objectivity of Scripture, the very integrity of revelation.

The third element is related to the first two. One of the great claims, even shibboleths, of our era is what is called the scientific method of verification. Truth-claims have to be tested by criteria that either validate or falsify them,

and the application of this method has led to all the benefits of modern science. It is often forgotten, of course, that
many of the advances in science seem to have as much to
do with imaginative, almost mystical leaps of recognition,
as with the verification process itself. However, in science,
hunches or revelations are tested to destruction. So, science
seems to be about something actual, verifiable, and, ultimately, beneficial, while religion seems to be increasingly
elusive and beyond verification, and the passions it arouses
seem to be more damaging than beneficial to humanity.
The result of these tendencies, however gradual and unadmitted, is to make religion lose some of its plausibility, so
that it becomes increasingly marginal.

The fourth element in this cumulative erosion of religious confidence has been contributed by our increasing
awareness of other religions. When I was a boy, we could
safely ignore them—they were the primitive superstitions of
the subject peoples of the British Empire. At their best
they were seen as the childhood stage of religious development, while at their worst they were thought of as
positively demonic. The situation has altered radically.
One of the consequences of the dismantling of the British
Empire was the emergence of Britain as a multi-ethnic
society, so that real encounter with other faiths is un-
avoidable, even in an insular society like ours. We can
detect a variety of influences here. Perhaps the most
important is the guilt Christians felt about the fate of the
Jewish people and their own part in that ancient tragedy.
Another aspect was the emergence of the counter-culture
in the 1960s and 1970s that led to a new appraisal of
Eastern religions, such as Buddhism and Hinduism, and,
in the USA in particular, a growing respect for the
spiritism of the native American community. Of course,

the rising impact of Islam has added another very turbulent ingredient to the multi-ethnic pot. The result is a situation of religious pluralism that has further served to diminish the plausibility of any single religion. Religion has become multiform in our society, making it easier for commentators to downgrade and relativize its significance. In the spiritual supermarket, no one thing is better than anything else.

The final element in this cumulative process is the ideology of tolerance that has emerged in Western democracies over the last 400 years. There are people who do not think tolerance is a virtue and, until fairly recently, most people would have agreed with them. Most of our ancestors believed in their own truth and fought for it to prevail. People were sickened by the strife and bloodshed that resulted, and tolerance emerged as a practical way of keeping ourselves from each others' throats. In time, most religions and philosophies were offered the protection of the law, provided they acknowledged the rights of others. This external tolerance has been interiorized to become a unifying principle in our society. Indeed, one of the most intriguing things about the Salman Rushdie affair has been the way modern tolerant humanists have been surprised by the pre-tolerant passions of the Islamic community. However, in a society in which everything is tolerated, nothing is rated particularly highly. So this civilized agreement only serves to diminish further the plausibility of any single religious claim.

The result of this cumulative process, which has led to what we call modernity, relativism or pluralism, has been the creation of a high level of cognitive anxiety in our society about religious claims. In the spiritual supermarket, how are we to find our way down the packed corridors and make our life choices?

There are two extreme reactions to the position we find ourselves in. The first is what we might call absolute brand loyalty or fundamentalism. Brand loyalists simply ignore the new culture. They do not say, 'this is the brand I prefer' and stick to it, but 'this is the right brand and everything else on offer in here will poison you if you consume it'. The advantages of this position are obvious. At a stroke it removes cognitive anxiety and gives profound personal assurance, but it makes it very difficult to relate to other shoppers, most of whom it consigns to destruction. As a position it can only be preserved by walling ourselves into a ghetto of the mind. Theologically it is suspect because it seems to take little account of natural theology, the sense of God working throughout creation and throughout human history, no matter how fumblingly human beings stretch out towards him. The opposite reaction to this is absolute relativism and it, too, has a technical name, *Pyrrhonism*, which is the complete incapacity to make any choices whatsoever. According to the absolute relativist, nothing is better than anything else, including, presumably, the philosophical basis on which that judgement is made, because, if all judgements are relative, then the judgement that all judgements are relative must itself be relative. Neither absolute brand loyalty nor absolute relativism feels wise to me, but Christians ought to understand the pressures that lead people to adopt these positions if they are to preach an intelligent gospel in today's world.

There is a tendency in human nature for each generation to think its difficulties are unique, but discomfort is an inevitable aspect of truth-seeking. I believe that the Anglican Church is particularly well-placed to respond to the pains of pluralism and modernity. For many years we have been a pluralist culture in our own right, and discord is part of our way of life. In fact, this is something that has characterized Christianity from the beginning. It goes back to Jesus, who told us that he came to bring not peace but a sword and that we would be guided into all the truth. I think there is a connection between these two sayings, as truth-seeking involves us inescapably in conflict. As we have already observed, when human beings search for truth, they come up against the phenomenon of truths that are in opposition to each other. Most of the conflicts that characterize human history are not about the battle between right and wrong, truth and error, but the battle between opposing rights or opposing truths. This is summed up by a poem from Boethius: 'This discord in the pact of things, this endless war twixt truth and truth, that singly hold yet give the lie to him who seeks to yoke them both'.[1] This gives rise to what philosophers call the 'dialectical' model. A truth is stated, a thesis; this is immediately opposed by a contradictory truth, an antithesis; these two struggle or wrestle together and, from the struggle, there emerges a kind of synthesis that is not just an artificial unity of the two opposing truths, but something that transcends them both.

In politics, for instance, there are some people who feel instinctively that freedom is the highest value: it enables human beings to flourish, to develop, to prosper, to express themselves. They are drawn towards a commitment to freedom that, at its most extreme, can lead to a level of competition that is almost Darwinian in its intensity, in which only the fittest survive. Other people emphasize and value, with equal passion, the truth of equality: that all people are born equal, that it is wrong in the eyes of God that there should be gulfs between nations, between individuals, circumstances in which some flourish and some suffer, some have and some have not. People who instinctively and passionately gravitate towards this truth will work to establish societies where inequalities are ironed out and, in so doing, will limit certain human freedoms because they believe that the good of equality transcends all the political goods offered by other systems.

There is an ecology of ideas that struggle and balance each other. We see this focused institutionally in the various types of parliamentary democracy that have evolved in the West. Such democracies base their structures on the very notion of conflict. They believe that truth- and power-seeking are inescapable but perilous pursuits, so they have built into their structures checks and balances against one truth lording it over other truths in a totalitarian way.

Democracies have two important principles embedded in their structures. The first is the principle of *opposition*, the conviction that any statement or thesis or encapsulation of the truth must be opposed with equal passion by a statement of the opposite or conflicting truth. The principle of opposition is seen at work more dramatically in the British Parliament than in American political structures, but it is important to each of them. The second principle is that the people have the right to *reverse* the direction of government, from time to time, by throwing it out at an election. Opposition and reversibility are important democratic principles rooted in the knowledge that truth-seeking is an inescapably turbulent human process, intrinsically painful and uncomfortable.

If we turn to theology, or ecclesiology, we discover that the same law holds. Religious people and institutions have no route to truth that miraculously avoids the need for clash and conflict. Of course, many religious institutions believe that they have this infallibility, but their claim is easily contested. The one thing that we can say with confidence about all religious claims is that they are contestable and have been and will go on being contested. Two approaches to the struggle for truth seem permanently in contention within the Christian community. They are the principles of *revelation* and *reason*.

By 'revelation' we mean the knowledge or truth that seems to come from above, comes directly from God and has a givenness and objectivity about it. As we have already seen, people debate both the nature and the content of revelation and the means whereby it was given. Nevertheless, at the heart of the Christian tradition is the claim that something came from God that is self-evident, has its own authority within itself and has to be submitted to. We might call this the Catholic substance Tillich mentioned. It sits there like a great rock that dominates the landscape.

The other important reality in religious history is that of reason, with its critical, probing, questioning dynamic. Reason often seems to be in conflict with the claims of revelation: it is always questioning, seeking to discover more about revelation; indeed, it may often appear to contradict the claims of revelation. If revelation is a supernatural reality, reason is a natural reality. If the specific focus of the supernatural revelation is Scripture, then the specific location of the principle of reason is clearly the turbulent, questioning mind of humanity.

In Anglican experience this conflict, this 'endless war twixt truth and truth' is expressed in three strands of spiritual reality. These three strands or cords are woven together, in theory, into a rope that is not easily broken, but, in fact, the strands often seem to unravel and jerk and wriggle away from each other, rather than binding together. The strands are Scripture, tradition and reason.

Scripture has to be interpreted and interpretation is best done over a long period by as many people as possible, giving rise to a broad and deep river of experience that we call tradition; and always there is the individual reason, the private thinker tackling, questioning the authority of Scripture and its extension, tradition. These three elements that are strongest when wound together tend to separate in actual Christian experience. This is an inescapable human reality: the need for companionship and support, even in truth-seeking, leads to the grouping of the like-minded, those congenial with one another. Roughly speaking, we could say that those who emphasize Scripture to the exclusion, or at the expense, of tradition, group themselves under the evangelical Protestant banner, while Catholics emphasize the continuity of tradition, with Scripture being seen as part of tradition rather than the fount of it. Those who exclusively emphasize reason tend to end up in Liberal Protestantism, Unitarianism or even atheism, because if we emphasize human reason to the exclusion of revelation, we can end up excluding the supernatural altogether.

The fascinating thing about Anglicanism, however, is that it did not separate in this way. Rather than becoming a party committed to a single idea, it became more like a parliament in which rival parties jockeyed for power. The Anglican Reformation was a conservative revolution. It retained much from the past, though it absorbed many of the new ideas that were in ferment on the Continent, and it went on evolving for several hundreds of years; indeed, it can be said to be evolving still. We are an inclusive Church, we lack the cutting edge of sectarianism. The price we pay for our inclusiveness is a permanent tension among ourselves and a frequent inability to decide issues, because there is a stand-off between the rival parties. We are a bit like certain European parliaments where there are several parties that all discount each other during elections and end up grid-locked into political indecision. This is the particular weakness of Anglicanism, the discomfort that is intrinsic to its nature. It is a weakness that is exacerbated by the way ecclesial authority is diffused throughout the Anglican Communion.

The Anglican Church is a family or fellowship (in Greek *koinonia*, in Latin *communio*) of autonomous provinces. Each province is self-governing within certain limits. For instance, each province is free to decide its own attitude to marriage discipline or the way it organizes the selection and ordination of candidates for the ministry, but it is not free to decide, for instance, to abandon the doctrine of the Holy Trinity or the divine nature of Christ. In other words, it has the freedom to control its own attitude to secondary or tertiary theological matters, but not matters of primary importance. The difficulty is in deciding what is primary and what is secondary.

There have been constant predictions about the end or break up of Anglicanism. There *are* strains and tensions in the Anglican Communion, and we acknowledge these without fudging them, but we also recognize that these tensions and disagreements are part of the very nature of Anglicanism and we affirm that they help to define our distinctiveness, so we must go on living with them, no matter how painful it is. A recent example of this is the aftermath of the Church of England's decision on 11 November 1992 to ordain women to the priesthood. The decision clearly increased these strains and it marked the end for some people; it was a step too far. Another way of reading the situation is to see it as one more frontier in the Church's pilgrimage through history. Some will go over it reluctantly, some gladly, but in time it will be seen as a staging post on the journey, not an end point.

There are two perceptions emerging in Anglican thought, two insights that will be useful to the whole Christian community as they struggle in their traditions with the different claims of truth. The first is the doctrine of *reception* and the second is *contextuality*.

When a new idea is mooted or some apparently radical departure from tradition is proposed, it takes time, sometimes a long time, for such an idea or proposal to be 'received' by everyone. Some are quick to receive new ideas, some are slow. The process of 'reception' can be disconcerting, as brake and accelerator pull against each other, but in time the new thing is either abandoned or finally received by all—and the body of the Church moves on.

Linked to the idea of reception is the idea of contextuality. Each part of the Church is set in a particular context and that context affects the Church's social and theological agenda. An issue that is hot in America may be absolutely cold in Africa, and vice versa. Polygamy, for instance, is a topic of intense interest and importance in Africa, but it is not an issue in Scotland. By the same token, women's ordination is a hot issue in Europe and America, though it is hardly even on the agenda of the Church in Melanesia, and so on.

The mature wisdom that underlies the recognition of the importance of reception and contextuality is something to admire and celebrate, because it describes the way things actually happen. This is how people are and how the Church is. It is liberating to belong to a body of faith that recognizes the complexity of truth-seeking and does not insist that everyone should march in step to the same tune.

Anglicans love freedom and space. As the Coverdale Psalter reminds us, 'Thou has set our feet in a large room'. Anglicans believe that this allows the many-sidedness of truth to be expressed. We have already acknowledged that this freedom, this spaciousness, brings with it an acute sense of discomfort, because no position, no point of view, goes unchallenged for long. This makes us slow to judge because we believe that people should not rush to judgement *and* because we find it difficult to get our act together sufficiently to make judgements that stick. However, we do not endure this discomfort simply out of weakness, but because we have accepted as fundamental the necessity and purifying value of conflict as an inescapable part of the theological and spiritual enterprise. To the outsider this can appear baffling; it can look as though anything goes, that we can believe what we like. That, of course, is far from being the case; we have our common convictions. Nevertheless, we have always preferred to express our beliefs in worship and in liturgy rather than in iron-clad, bolted and padlocked confessional statements and credal formularies. As we worship, so we believe. We are only together on our knees.

This is why Anglicanism is an inappropriate environment for the sort of people who like their philosophical universe to consist of hard objects with sharp edges. We have our convictions, our certainties, but we confine them to the central core of the gospel message and sit more lightly to the institutional arrangements that organized churches find it convenient to adopt. People who like everything stamped with the divine mandate will be happier elsewhere. In recent months, some people temperamentally unsuited to Anglicanism have left us, to the blowing of trumpets and the flashing of cameras. What is rarely recorded, however, is the traffic in the other direction, which, particularly in the USA, greatly exceeds it.

If we return to the spiritual supermarket and the uncomfortable choices and tensions of modernity and pluralism, we can see that Anglicans will be in a good position to handle them, partly because we are used to living with conflict, partly because we have learned that truth is dynamic. We can be certain that there will be a variety of responses to the modern situation and that none will be absolutely perfect. That, too, is of the nature of the life of faith.

I would like to propose a personal strategy for responding to the modern predicament. The first thing to note is that, however uncomfortable this time is, God is in it because God is a God of history. We need a theology that will affirm, as well as analyse and criticize cultural development. If our God is a God of history, then part of our discipleship involves us in a dialogue, even a controversy, with history, but no flight from it into some transhistorical haven of timelessness. Each generation of Christians has felt the pressure of cultural and philosophical development, but the best of them have met the challenge by preaching to the times and not fleeing from them.

So we must learn, somehow, to acknowledge the times in which we live, even when this is painful, and discover something of the freedom of God in them. Nevertheless, we must be bold enough to make choices, remembering that every choice is a rejection, an act of judgement. We do not have to be uncritical in our response to modernity and its discontents.

One of the most interesting sub-themes in theology and philosophy today is the challenge that is being put to many of the assumptions that form the foundations of contemporary religious pluralism. The philosopher Alasdair MacIntyre has been leading a charge against many of the developments in post-Enlightenment humanistic philosophy and Bishop Lesslie Newbigin is doing the same thing in theology. We must have the confidence to challenge some of the prevailing norms in our culture and we must be prepared to make our own choices with confidence. Nevertheless, we ought to practise cognitive modesty as confidence is not the same thing as arrogance. We should learn, too, to distinguish between the uniqueness of Christ and the non-uniqueness of Christianity. The historian Herbert Butterfield sums this up perfectly: 'Hold to Jesus and for the rest be uncommitted'.

# Part II

# 5

## Beyond Nationalism

Christian theology is a system of paradoxes. This is not because Christian theologians have a weakness for intellectual games, but because human experience itself is highly paradoxical and Christian theology is a reflection of human experience. As we have already acknowledged, paradoxes are difficult, uncomfortable things to live with. This is one of the reasons that there is so much conflict in human experience. Most of us have minds that are too narrow to embrace the whole range of truth, so we opt for a partial truth, claim infallibility for our sect and excommunicate all the others. We have already noticed that most human conflict arises not between truth and error, right and wrong, but between truth and truth. The opposite of a truth is not a lie but an opposing truth. All the Christian paradoxes illumine the human situation, but in this chapter we are thinking about politics and there is one foundational paradox in Christianity that is particularly apposite to this discussion. I want to begin with a brief exposition of it.

What theologians used to call the doctrine of man, and now, more appropriately, call the doctrine of human nature is a profound example of Christian paradox. The Christian account of humanity is both positive and negative, hopeful and pessimistic, trusting and suspicious.

The first element in our doctrine of human nature is what is misleadingly called original sin. The term is misleading, because the word 'sin' suggests an intentional act, something for which we are responsible. St Augustine was the greatest and most eloquent exponent of this version of original sin. He taught that the primordial sin of Adam and Eve tainted the whole human race. This was the originating offence, which has been handed on to humanity like a genetic disorder, and for which we are born guilty, born accountable. Now we do not have to accept St Augustine's version of original sin to find value in the concept. We have already noted that Christian paradoxes are based, not upon theory, but upon observation, and the doctrine of original sin is the most empirical of the Christian doctrines, if we can forget the Augustinian glosses and the mythic embroidery of Adam and Eve in the Garden of Eden. A clinical observation of human nature soon informs us that there is a bias or tendency in human nature that distorts and vitiates all our relationships and institutions. Original sin is the theological equivalent of Murphy's Law, which is that if a thing *can* go wrong it *will*. In human experience, things invariably go wrong. Even the most loving relationships have their moments of strife, anger and pettiness. Magnified on the collective scale, this tendency accounts for the violence and strife of our history. However we account for it, there is something in us that is resistant to the self-effacement and unselfishness that living in community calls for.

I am not offering any kind of theory of origin for this melancholy fact, but fact it is. Call it ignorance, irrationality or original selfishness, it is obvious that each of us is inescapably locked within our own selfhood from which we look out upon others and the world. We are, by definition, the centre of our own universe. William Temple called this the parable of perspective. I see the world from my own control tower. I am the centre of my universe in a quite inescapable way. I cannot get out of my own skin. I cannot, except imaginatively, get into anyone else's. I see things from behind my own eyes. This physical fact brings with it psychic and spiritual correlatives, so that I become the centre and the maker of value, the judge and tester of what is right and what is wrong. Equally, everyone else in the universe is doing the same; you are the centre of your own universe. I am a walk-on part in your little soap opera, whereas I am the star in my own. Many complicated results flow from this originating self-centredness, but human conflict is the most intractable consequence. The New Testament paradigm for original sin is the crucifixion. The crucifixion of the just man is a parable of the terrible consequences of this mysterious flaw in our nature.

Now the doctrine of original sin, this deeply pessimistic assessment of human nature, has profound political consequences. If we lay emphasis upon this end of the doctrine of human nature, it will lead us towards political conservatism. Given the volatile and disordered nature of humanity, according to this approach, the best system is one that will keep society in some kind of equilibrium, so it will be suspicious of change. It will also be suspicious of strangers. We can, perhaps, learn to cope with our own sort whose vagaries we understand, but the exotic variations of original sin found in foreigners is too much for us, so we will be wary of them, maybe even develop theories about them, and, on the whole, will prefer not to associate with them.

Another characteristic of the politics of original sin is that it emphasizes the rule of law. It is suspicious of human nature and seeks to create checks upon its abuses of power. It will prefer structures that prize order above freedom. It will prefer the abuses of order to the abuses of freedom.

The third characteristic of the politics of original sin is that its political rhetoric is minatory, given to warning people about the dangers that beset them. It will inculcate a certain wariness, warn people about the dangers of life. Indeed, its attitude to life is not unlike the Ministry of Health's attitude to sex in a post-AIDS society: be careful, practise safe politics, do not take any risks. One of the paradoxes of original sin is that its very pessimism has had positive and beneficial effects on our political evolution. Reinhold Niebuhr captured the situation in his best epigrammatic style when he said that 'man's capacity for justice makes democracy possible, while man's capacity for injustice makes democracy essential'. It is because we know that we are capable of terrible abuses of one another that we have developed structures to check the abuse of power. One of the fruits of the politics of original sin is constitutional democracy, with its two principles of opposition and reversibility. Every government must be officially opposed and every electoral decision must be reversible. These undoubted benefits are essentially negative and cautionary. The political system that emphasizes this side of human nature will tend to be static and unadventurous, preferring the devil it knows to delights of which it has no experience.

Original sin is one end of the paradox of the Christian doctrine of human nature. It has to be balanced by the other end, which we can call original blessing or original righteousness. Humanity is made in God's image. It has a capacity for growth and evolution. It can co-operate with the action of God in history. There is a developmental energy in human history and it is this characteristic that most clearly differentiates us from the animal kingdom. Unlike animals, we are not fixed, finished creatures, programmed to an endless repetition of the same life cycle. Because humanity is an open rather than a closed system, there is endless potential for growth and development. A Jewish theologian pointed out that when God made the animals and inanimate nature he said they were good, but when he made humanity he did not say it was good. This was because humanity was not complete, it was in process, it was still being created, it was on the way. This is why human history is punctuated with surprises, as well as sorrows, with new and exciting developments, as well as with ancient miseries.

The New Testament paradigm of this end of the paradox of human nature is, of course, the resurrection of Jesus. The resurrection proclaims God's possibility, which is limitless. Christ tells his grieving disciples to leave the graveyard where they laid him and go into the Galilee of their own future. The risen Christ calls his followers to look ahead, not back, to be hopeful of the future, not nostalgic for the past. So, the politics of original blessing will be progressive and eager for change, it will be expectant about history, seeing its benefits, seeing it as more opportunity than curse. The politics of original blessing is the politics of possibility and one of its characteristics will be its liberationism. It will look upon the marvellous variety of human nature in a wondering and approving way. It will see pluralism as something to celebrate, not something to deplore. Dazzled by the variety of traditions, customs, and moral and spiritual systems in human history, it will be magnanimous in its affirmation of the human capacity to see things differently. So the politics of original blessing will be the politics of celebration, not suspicion.

On the whole, British politics has been a politics of original sin rather than original blessing. The realism of the British political tradition has given to our history a certain predictability and steadiness. We have avoided, because of our instinctive caution, many of the headier Utopian experiments of other countries. Why this should be so I cannot say exactly. It is probably a combination of the weather and the fact that we are an island. It would be difficult to overestimate the significance of British insularity. One commentator has pointed out that to the average Englishman, the English Channel is wider than the Atlantic. Our politicians tend to look more towards the United States, which is further away, than to Europe, which is on our doorstep. We feel a kind of residual relationship to the USA. It was one of our colonies and still speaks our language. Of course, it is a more significant nation than we are, but we are still proud of our connection. We feel a bit like the vicar in a Trollope novel whose daughter has married a duke. However we account for it, the British political system fits the politics of original sin pretty closely. There has been a traditional mistrust of foreigners, comically present in certain sections of the English Tory party. It was highly entertaining to see Sir Edward Heath on the television telling the nation that Lady Thatcher hated foreigners. In that she is extremely English.

Another characteristic of the politics of original sin, which seems to be represented in the British system, is its suspicion of freedom of information. Ours is a secretive society. Our political leaders seem to think that we cannot be trusted with information that concerns us. Our system is the most secretive of all the Western democracies. The cause probably lies in the suspiciousness and protectiveness that characterizes a system that is wary of human nature and the deepest instinct of which is to rein it in rather than run the dangers of letting it off the leash.

A wise politics will not so much be a balance between both poles of the Christian paradox as a judicious use of both. A variety of motoring images suggest themselves here. If we think of the human enterprise as a vehicle moving along the road of time, it is obvious that it will require both brakes and accelerator, but the main *purpose* of the vehicle is locomotion. We need the brakes, but the fact remains that the braking system on a car is secondary to its primary purpose, which is movement.

There are many people who resist this idea of movement through time. They are usually people of a profoundly pessimistic and nostalgic temperament who desire to turn the engine off and park in a pleasant lay-by of their own choosing. Evelyn Waugh was a supreme example of this breed. His whole life was a search for what R. S. Thomas has called 'the glimpsed good place permanent'. He sought it everywhere and found it nowhere, not even in the Roman Catholic Church. Waugh, for all his Scottish bloodlines, was a quintessentially English character. There is something entertaining yet repellent about the classic English reactionary, who hates foreigners and progress and wishes to return to an idealized version of Merrie England, with the peasants dancing on the village green, while the pipe-smoking vicar, leaning on the churchyard wall, gazes benignly upon them as he looks forward to his monthly dinner with the local squire at the big house outside the village. There is a magazine I have never seen in Britain, but see quite often in the USA, that exemplifies this freeze-dried version of English history. It is called *This England* and it is clearly published for export only. My Anglophiliac father-in-law takes it. It is filled with nostalgic articles about cricket and cathedral towns and the great public schools, but, beneath the whimsy and nostalgia, there is an ugly subtext that bemoans the changing face of England, with its ethnic and religious pluralism and the looming threat of the new Europe. It is obvious that this spirit flourishes in political circles in England today.

It is difficult not to feel a certain amusement at this vision of Merrie England, but there is something about it that is profoundly unattractive, because it represents a position of stubborn ignorance, a refusal to countenance new possibilites or new developments. An African priest captured the lopsidedness of this approach to living institutions when he described the Church of England as a most peculiar machine, because it had the engine of a lawnmower and the brakes of a juggernaut.

Before leaving this image, let me suggest another metaphor for the past—that of the driving mirror. Wise drivers check the mirror frequently, knowing that, in order to move forward safely, we have to keep an eye on what is behind. Reactionaries, if they drive at all, drive with their eyes permanently fixed on what is behind them, while those who have no interest in the past drive without a mirror. The judicious politician, however, knows the value of history but knows, too, that it is about movement. Winston Churchill, who is frequently used as a champion by reactionaries, is a very good example of a conservative with an almost mystical passion for British history who was yet able to discern the future and move towards it. Dr Paul Addison, the Head of Modern History at the University of Edinburgh, has written a book entitled

*Churchill on the Home Front, 1900–55* (Pimlico 1993). His book is full of examples of Churchill's ability to look back as he moved forward. It is not generally known, for instance, that, as early as 1911, he put forward a plan for a radical devolution of powers throughout Britain. He proposed that the United Kingdom should be divided into ten areas, having regard to geographical, racial and historical considerations. If Churchill's plan had been adopted, it would have turned the United Kingdom into a federal state with some resemblance to the United States, Canada or Australia. Addison points out that it was too imaginative and enlightened a plan to match the political realities. Churchill was equally daring and imaginative in his attitude towards Europe. In another fascinating historical study, *Never Again: Britain 1945–51*, Peter Hennessy describes a great rally at the Albert Hall in 1947 to launch the movement for a united Europe. In a characteristic speech, Churchill said this:

> We shall only save ourselves . . . by rejoicing together in that glorious treasure of literature, of remembrance, of ethics, of thought and toleration belonging to all, which is the true inheritance of Europe . . . It is said with truth that this involves some sacrifice or merger of national sovereignty. But it is also possible and not less agreeable to regard it as a gradual assumption by all the nations concerned of that larger sovereignty that can also protect the diverse and distinct customs and characteristics and the national traditions, all of which under totalitarian systems . . . would certainly be blotted out for ever.[1]

Visionary politicians capture the imagination of their people because they see the future and lay hold of it, while at the same time understanding their own history and its often paralysing effect. Wise leaders will balance a necessary caution towards human institutions, knowing what they know about the weaknesses of human nature, with the largeness of heart that affirms human aspirations and the strong urge in human history to transcend the past and move bravely into the future.

The dilemma that faces us today is to move from the confines of nationalism to supra-nationalism, to sacrifice some elements of sovereignty for the sake of what Churchill called 'that larger sovereignty which can also protect our diverse and distinctive customs and our national traditions'. It is often forgotten that nationalism, which is becoming the new stumbling block in the way of these new and larger unities, itself represents a previous development in dealing with the human dilemma. Nations are not given things, they are not facts of nature, they represent a stage in human evolution, a subduing of ethnic factions into a larger whole. The nation was an assertion of rational control over that state of nature that was inherently factionalist and tribal. In their modern European guise, the emergence of nations in the sixteenth century represented a challenge to the autocratic supra-nationalism of the Roman Catholic Church. Only in the sixteenth and seventeenth century, with the rise of strong European monarchies, did modern nations as we know them today come into being. Many of these nationalist groupings have been inherently unstable since the beginning. The Austro-Hungarian empire managed to maintain its rule over nine different nationalities until the First World War. The Russian empire achieved a similar stability until 1989. What we are seeing in Eastern Europe today is the retribalizing of unities that were imposed from above rather than voluntarily embraced from below.

Nationalism represents both a development and a threat to human nature. It captures both poles of the paradox we have been describing. It points to the need for a larger unity in which the volatility and factionalism that is intrinsic to human groupings is transcended by a larger loyalty. It has to be admitted immediately, however, that each stage in human political evolution is inherently unstable as all human institutions are caught in the tension between original sin and original blessing, between human irrationality and the human ability to transcend its own irrationalism.

Human beings live with dilemmas. Our current dilemma is to decide whether the new Europe is the next best step for humankind or is to be seen as yet another dangerous concentration of power. There is no reason, of course, why it cannot be seen as both. Entering into the new unity does not abrogate the need for vigilance.

In a remarkable speech[2] delivered at the Harvard Club of New York in March 1992, Walter Wriston, former Chairman of CitiBank, pointed out that new information technology has rendered the previous state of evolution of nations problematic, if not meaningless: 'In the past, sovereignty and nationhood had been based largely on the idea of territoriality, but the information revolution makes the assertion of territorial control more difficult in certain ways and less relevant in others'. He points out that, 'radio waves have never respected frontiers, and from an altitude of 36,000 kilometres, national boundaries are singularly inconspicuous'. The paradigm of this new supra-national reality is the money market. He points out that, just as Eddison failed to foresee that his phonograph would have any commercial value, the men and women who tied the world together with telecommunications did not fully realize that they were building the infrastructure of a global market-place.

Wriston maintains that the information standard has replaced the gold standard, and that technology has made us a global community in the literal sense of the word. This means that the world can no longer be understood as a collection of national economies. An electronic infrastructure that binds the world together and the efficiency of conventional transportation have created a single global economy. The old political boundaries of nation states are being made obsolete by an alliance of commerce and technology. Political borders, long the cause of wars, are becoming porous. In the face of this fascinatingly complicated human phenomenon, the old hierarchies and structures of sovereignty have to learn that they can no longer operate as once they did. We desperately need a new model of political co-operation, a new paradigm, to embrace the globalization of the human community, while maintaining our vigilance against its possible corruption. Wriston maintains that politicians can learn a great deal from new managerial theories. He says that, instead of the old military model of hierarchical organization, there is emerging what he calls flatter structures, designed for the faster response times needed to serve dynamic global markets.

The vision of the future presented by the new Europe can be incredibly attractive, because, on the one hand, it affirms the need to transcend our local rivalries in order to achieve larger unities, but, on the other hand, it offers us limitless possibilities for a genuine diffusion of power and responsibility across the globe. In response to the Wriston lecture, Henry Grunwald,[3] former Editor-in-Chief of *Time* Incorporated and US Ambassador to Austria, pointed out that Riccardo Petrella, a man he describes as an imaginative Eurocrat, visualizes a future situation in which he sees a landscape of highly developed city regions, resembling the old, pre-national Hanseatic cities, linked together through transnational business. Such cities as Barcelona, Lyons, Milan, Strasbourg and Stuttgart are already co-operating closely without going through their central governments. Thus, the post-national economic geography, he believes, will look very much like the pre-national one.

If enough of us summon up the necessary courage, we could unite the best of our past with the best of the future in a new human system that embraces the global community, but, at the same time, respects our need to be part of accessible structures and our aversion to distant hierarchical models of government. It seems to me, therefore, that the Christian Church should be encouraging its people to dream dreams and to see visions, to move into this new future, to accept the reality of the gobal community and to make it work for humanity, by combining it with a new politics of miniaturization, in which human beings participate intimately in the decisions that affect their own destiny. It is a heady and Utopian vision that appeals to those of us who are closer to the original blessing end of the paradox of human nature, but we must also be careful to pay attention to the need for vigilance. It seems to be the case that Scotland is more open to this vision, probably because its experience of current British nationalism has not been wholly positive. In the larger unity of the new Europe, Scotland might rediscover its own virtues and, at the same time, rediscover value in being part of larger unities that include but transcend Britain.

If the Scottish Church is to embrace the possibilities of this new future, it can only avoid the accusation of hypocrisy if it allows its power to work upon its own structures. Severely hierarchical systems, whether on the monarchical or the bureaucratic model, will be unconvincing exponents of the new order if it is not seen to be influencing its own structures. For all the apparent friendliness and co-operation that exists between its various branches, the Scottish Church is a flourishing example of ecclesiological tribalism. As often happens, it is the world that brings the good news to the Church and challenges it to rethink its own structures.

I believe the Scottish Church should embrace the vision of the new Europe, but this can only be done with integrity if there is a commitment to a new and more radical ecumenism. Not the present ecumenism of diplomacy and cordial relations between sovereign states, but a new prophetic ecumenism that will challenge current ecclesiologies to recognize that there has been a parallel movement of globalization in the Christian community and that Christians, particularly lay Christians, no longer think of themselves as subjects of particular allegiances, but as members of a new humanity in Christ that transcends the old order. 'Behold I make all things new', says the Lord, but for those obsessively clinging to old systems, the divine promise brings discomfort and disturbance. However, that is the way it has always been since the risen Christ told his first followers not to hang around looking for him in the graveyard of the past, but to follow him into Galilee, into the future.

# 6

## The Cry of the Homeless

We have already acknowledged that Christians believe that God speaks to us through Scripture and our own historic situation. In fact, if we are true to the best in our tradition, we do not separate these two vehicles of divine guidance. Rather, Scripture becomes an instrument that helps us to discern God's action in our own history.

How, though, do we hear God speaking to us in our day? In Chapter 2, we looked at an incident in Matthew's Gospel, chapter 15—Jesus, on a missionary journey with his apostles, is encountered by a pagan woman who asks for his help. I would like us to remember several elements of the encounter. First, there is what we might describe as an insider group, consisting of Jesus and his apostles. This group, bound up in its own life, is intent on a particular mission under the guidance of God. It is sent to the lost sheep of the house of Israel. It is for Jews only, and it is unconcerned by, indeed it is almost oblivious to, those outside that particular community. The second element in the story is the existence of a needy outsider; an outsider in at least two senses, because she is a woman and a gentile. She claims the help of the insider group by crying to Jesus Christ, who is at its centre—'Lord help me'. The third element in the story is the resistance of the insider group to this petition from the margins. Those around Jesus beg him to send her away for she is crying after them and disturbing their peace. The fourth element in the story is that Jesus, while he is at first disposed to take the insider's line, nevertheless listens to the woman and finally agrees to help, and her daughter is healed.

Deep in the story a major human and theological event has occurred. The healing of the woman's daughter is itself a major event, but the event is historically significant, as we noted earlier, because it is the first hint of that universal mission to the gentiles that was to become the characteristic of the Christian message. So, we have an extraordinary narrative here: an insider group, satisfied that it was doing the will of God, is summoned by God by means of an outsider, a woman on the margins far beyond its concern, to do and hear a new thing. According to this story from Scripture, God speaks to us from the outside, God addresses us from the margins of our own concern. That is why it is easy to miss what God is saying to us. However, if we on the inside listen and are attentive to those on the margins we will hear God address us and invite us to act. It is obvious, therefore, that any insiders' group, religious or political, is in danger of being so bound up in its own life that it does not hear God speaking to it from the edge. We must constantly ask ourselves, therefore, who are our outsiders, who is on the margin in our society, because that is where we will find God.

The point of this theological prologue is that the Church must be attentive to those on the outside of society and the Church because God is likely to be addressing it from its margins rather than from its own centre. Let us turn now to sketch in some principles and assumptions that characterize Christian thinking on social policy.

In the previous chapter we tried to understand what Christians call 'original sin', though we noted that the term is misleading and can be dangerously misapplied. It is probably best summed up in an aphorism of Immanuel Kant's: 'Out of timber so crooked as that from which man is made nothing entirely straight can be built'. In other words, there is a flaw intrinsic to human nature that distorts and biases all its relationships and institutions. We can call that flaw chronic self-regard, primordial incompetence, or original sin. This innate ability to distort and twist things becomes particularly marked in our power relations, which is the area we shall look at now.

Lord Acton said, 'Power tends to corrupt and absolute power corrupts absolutely' and this is certainly true, but even relative power is dangerous. Indeed, it may be more dangerous when it is disguised in some form. However we define it, it is in the nature of power to create preferential interest groups that take control and manage others for the benefit of themselves. I like Alasdair McIntyre's new version of Lord Acton's epigram: 'All power co-opts and absolute power co-opts absolutely'. The powerful, and that means the wealthy, those with their hands on the levers of political and economic power, create great force fields around themselves that suck power from others and, almost unconsciously, control and dictate to them. An obvious example of this phenomenon is the existence of the vast and unjust imbalance in world trade, whereby the developed world systematically subordinates the developing world to its own economic self-interest. Most developed institutions end up serving the interests of the powerful and create unjust dualisms in which those on the inside pay no attention to the interests of those on the outside.

However, if we remember the theological prologue with which we started, we see that the Christian gospel precisely reverses that standard. The gospel places God precisely outside our power systems. Scripture is quite explicit on the subject and nowhere more eloquently than in the famous passage in Philippians, chapter 2, to which we alluded in Chapter 1, where Paul tells us that God, the source and origin of all power, empties himself of it and assumes the form of a slave, thereby calling the Christian movement to a revolutionary reappraisal of all power structures. If we would follow God, as opposed to following our own *ideas* about God, then we must follow God outside the systems of power that characterize the world and find God among the powerless.

The situation that I have described, whereby the powerful accrue more and more power to themselves and pay less and less attention to the powerless, has led to two major responses from those who try to follow God's way, rather than the way of the world. The first response is prophecy. The prophet is the great accuser of the world, who points to its manifest injustices. Prophecy expresses God's anguish at the way the powerful abuse the powerless. Perhaps the archetypal act of prophecy in the Old Testament is the story of Nathan and King David. King David, the charming, charismatic darling of Israel, stole Bath-sheba, the wife of Uriah the Hittite, for himself. To hide his own shame, he had Uriah put in the front line of battle so that he might be slain. Nathan goes to David and tells him a story of the cruel depredations of a rich man upon a poor man. The story ignites David's wrath and he demands to know the name of such a monster. 'Thou art the man', says Nathan.

This is one of the inalienable duties of the Church. It is never a comfortable one and, in some societies, it can even be dangerous, as we have seen in South Africa and Central America, but it is the duty of the Church to become, in Desmond Tutu's words, the voice of the voiceless poor and the voice of the voiceless God. Prophecy, by definition, is rarely moderate in tone. In order to attract attention, it shocks. It is a kind of spiritual terrorism, designed to make people hear the voices of those they never meet, see people they never encounter, endlessly calling society to repentance and renewal.

It could be argued that prophecy is the sole task of the Church, that it should call the world to bring inside those on the outside and to bind the wounds of those it has cruelly injured. As a matter of record, the Church has never confined itself to prophecy; it has also sought to provide for those whom society has neglected. If prophecy is the first and most important response of the Church, then provision is the second and almost equally important response. Indeed, we could argue that the Church's provision of help for the helpless is itself prophetic. History, anyway, teaches us that the Church responded to God's identification with the poor by building hospitals, schools and homes for them, by what were known as works of mercy. Indeed, the Church down the centuries has always been closely identified with the practical provision of help for those society has thrust to the margins.

Nevertheless, provision of this sort in our day presents Christians with a profound philosophical and political problem. Largely in response to the pressures of the gospel, a social evolution took place in our society over the centuries. It was, admittedly, very slow, but by the end of the Second World War our nation committed itself to a doctrine of solidarity with the needy and the homeless that brought them into society as full members of the family for the first time. The Welfare State has been sneered at and, like any human institution, it has bred its own distortions and difficulties, but it was and remains a noble ideal. Society decided to assume the role of provision for the poor. Enormous social distinctions remained, of course, but there was an underlying conviction that we were part of the same family and that it was monstrous for some members of the family to be abandoned while the rest of us were comfortable.

The phenomenon of homelessness, for instance, was seen, not as an inevitable accompaniment of a market-driven social organization, but as an obvious injustice. To quote Pope John Paul II:

> Far from being a matter of simple lack or deprivation, to be homeless means to suffer from the deprivation or lack of something that is due. This consequently constitutes an injustice. Any ethical consideration of the housing problem must take this as its point of departure.[1]

That was one of the points of departure for the Welfare State. There were to be no outsiders, no disposable people, no tragic victims of the great social machine; all had become insiders. The Welfare State had its own inflationary dynamic built into it, of course, but it is a splendidly explicit realization of the Christian claim that we are all members one of another.

In recent years, however, we have seen a gradual process of reversal of this way of organizing care in our society. There is now considerable evidence that recent governments have sought to return to an earlier method of organizing society, whereby the needy become, not the responsibility of society as a whole (which, according to one view, does not really exist), but subject to the altruistic impulses of the individual. In other words, there is a distinct philosophical move towards the charitizing of provision in our society, to privatize care, to return to an atomic theory of the state that leaves care in the community to the arbitrary responses of the individual conscience.

There is considerable evidence that our society is reverting to the two nations excoriated by Benjamin Disraeli in the nineteenth century. According to the two nation theory of society, it is the duty of affluent and charitable citizens of the nation of plenty to go on soup runs and mercy flights to the nation of want. Given that kind of social dualism, Christians will certainly want to engage in these activities, but they must never lose sight of the fact that the system itself is wrong and that care for the needy is better undertaken by society as a whole, organized through professional structures, than left to the consciences and caprices of individuals. I remember when Shelter was founded at the end of the 1960s, Bruce Kenrick, whose idea it was, said, in response to someone who questioned the wisdom of doing for society what society ought to be doing for itself, that if a woman is lying at the roadside and the ambulance has not arrived, it is up to the passers-by to do what they can. That is why there has been a resurgence of charitable provision for the needy in our society in recent years, but it is fraught with difficulties.

Before I look at the specific problem posed by the housing crisis, let me make some general points about some of the consequences of the charitizing of care that we are witnessing in our society. As Chairman of the Edinburgh Voluntary Organisations Council, I have noticed that, in recent years, smaller charities of the sort that filled valuable interstices in the State's provision are now finding it very difficult to survive. For a couple of years in the Lothian Region of Scotland, fundraising of any sort by most organizations had to be put on hold because of The Sick Kids' Appeal. The Sick Children's Hospital in Edinburgh is a justly famous institution. Because of recent policies in the Health Service, it had to mount a massive appeal to extend and update its services. It was, of course, an irresistible and valid appeal, but it created a vacuum that sucked up money from all over the South East of Scotland that otherwise would have gone to other, less glamorous charities. I have noticed the same thing happening to another charity I am closely associated with, The Waverley Care Trust, that built and runs Milestone House, the first purpose-built hospice for people with AIDS in Britain. It is a marvellous place that really ought to be totally funded by Government because it provides both health and social care, but we have to raise approximately £380,000 a year to top up the grants we get from the Region and the Health Board. Raising money for AIDS projects is not easy anywhere, but there is considerable evidence that this obviously impressive place is in danger of drying up contributions to smaller AIDS charities.

Karl Popper talked about the unintended consequences of intentional social acts and there is considerable evidence to show that the provision of care by charities in our community promoted by the Government will make it increasingly difficult for the smaller, less glamorous, less well-known charities, to survive. When the national lottery, planned by the Government as a way of funding the arts, comes into play in a few years time it, too, will have a massively distorting effect on the funding of charities.

In conclusion, let me focus on a number of specific issues in the complicated field of housing. My main focus will be on the prophetic task of the Church, but that is not to imply that I believe the Church should not operate as a provider in this field.

The first and most dramatic aspect of the housing crisis that the Church should be focusing upon is homelessness, especially teenage homelessness. In the Pontifical Commission's *What Have You Done to Your Homeless Brother?*, the Pope writes:

> The situation of homelessness is the result of poverty and of social marginalization. In other words, it is the result of a whole series of economic, social, cultural, physical, emotional and moral factors that specifically bear down on those who have never been integrated into the current social system. Without substantial changes and modifications within societies marked by this fault, such integration will remain difficult or even impossible.[2]

Human beings habituate themselves to terrible evils and obvious inequities in their social systems. However, there is something peculiarly horrifying about the spreading incidence of absolute homelessness in our sophisticated society at the end of the second millennium.

According to the Scottish Federation of Housing Associations, there were 34,600 homeless applications to local authorities in Scotland in the year 1990-91. This represents an increase of 133 per cent over the last ten years. Of these, 23,155 households were actually assessed as homeless. The Federation believes that these official figures reveal only part of the problem. Many homeless individuals and childless couples do not apply to the authorities because they do not qualify for housing as homeless people. One in five couples with children lost their homes as a result of defaults in their mortgage repayments, which represents the fastest-growing cause of homelessness. Almost a quarter of all homeless applicants in 1990–91 were under twenty-five. One in 11 cases— 2,960 individuals in all—were under 18. About a third of homeless people have a background of being in care. Following Social Security changes in 1988, young people aged sixteen and seventeen have no automatic entitlement to Income Support, while those under twenty-five are entitled to a reduced level of Income Support. These changes to the Social Security system make it almost impossible for unemployed young people to live independently. It seems quite obvious to me that these facts are not only a national scandal but a challenge to the prophetic vocation of the Church. The uproar in the country at the Government's threat to close thirty-one pits in Britain in 1992 suggests that, when it is aroused, public opinion can change the mind of Government, however ideologically fixated it is.

The phenomenon of homelessness in our society should be as great an affront to the conscience of the nation as is the assassination of the mining industry. We know, however, that, because the homeless have become largely invisible to our eyes and they represent a complicated phenomenon, some but not all of which is directly due to the Government's policies, it is not easy for public opinion to be aroused in favour of their cause. All the more reason, therefore, why the Church should, in season and out of season, be the voice of these voiceless people and make society confront in them the consequences of its own policies. As the most horrifying aspect of the phenomenon of modern homelessness is provided by the number of youngsters on our streets, many of whom drift into crime and the sex industry in order to survive, the Church should campaign quite specifically for the restoration of benefit to sixteen and seventeen year olds, and of full benefit to the under twenty-fives. The intention behind the removal of these benefits in 1988 was to encourage families to take responsibility for their own children, but the result has been quite horrifying. It is as though we said to these children, your family does not want you, but neither do we, so just get lost.

We should also join with the Federation of Housing Associations in trying to persuade the Government to provide more social-rented houses. I am politically naive, I know, but I just cannot understand a society in which tens of thousands of people have no homes, in which 81,000 houses in Scotland alone are below the tolerable standard, 48,000 houses are unfit to live in due to damp, and over 300,000 houses are affected by dampness and condensation, yet we have a building industry that is standing idle because the Government refuses to allow local authorities to authorize house-building programmes. It is like ordering the fire brigade not to put out domestic fires in case it encourages people to smoke in bed. It would be comical if the consequences in human misery were not so heartbreaking.

These are areas in which the Church's prophetic role is clear cut. There are also ways in which the Church can both prophesy against current injustices and provide for the victims. A good example of the kind of thing that can be done is the London Churches Resettlement Agency, which was set up in 1984 in response to the problems of homeless single people in London. Let me quote from a recent report:

> The London Churches Resettlement Agency, an ecumenical organization, was set up in response to the growing housing problems of homeless single people. A

management development agency, the aim is to encourage local churches or church groups to respond to those needs by providing a range of small housing schemes. The LCRA believes that support of housing is the centrepiece of any strategy for helping those homeless single people who need both support and accommodation for a more stable life within the wider community, and that many congregations have the latent skills and resources to manage a small housing scheme. Such schemes may vary from a modest flat for two or three people, to cluster flats, group homes, etc. The Agency believes that some homeless people, making the move from institutions, are likely to need a degree of support, either within their new home or from the community generally. The Agency believes that local congregations could extend sensitive care and provide a means of tempering hostility from the community. The London Churches Resettlement Agency, through its teams of three workers, is able to give advice, support and guidance to groups throughout the setting up of the project.

Would it not be possible to set up agencies of this sort in cities and communities throughout Britain to encourage local churches to provide small projects that, cumulatively, could have a significant effect on the problem of homelessness in our country? The beauty of small schemes like this is that they are both friendly and achievable. They would not only contribute to the provision of housing for particularly vulnerable groups in our society, they would be prophetic signs to our churches that the one who had nowhere to lay his head still calls us from the wings to prepare a place for him.

# 7

# The Gospel of AIDS

The eruption of the AIDS virus on the world scene has had a precipitating effect upon moral and theological attitudes and many things have been brought to the surface by it, rather in the way an explosion underwater throws up dead fish, old tyres and Wellington boots on to the surface of a river or lake. A major epidemic or human tragedy on the scale of the AIDS epidemic raises absolutely basic questions about the nature of religion. The technical term for this area of concern is the doctrine of providence. In what sense does God, if God exists, provide for the moral support and guidance, perhaps even the moral reward and punishment, of human beings? In what sense is God active, if at all, in human history—in wars, in natural calamities, in plague, pestilence and famine? There seem to be at least five answers to these questions, and we will find that people, consciously or unconsciously, slot themselves somewhere along the line on which we find these answers.

The first answer is what we might call the 'personally rigged system'. There *is* a God and God has wired up the universe in such a way that actions of which he disapproves are visited with fateful consequences. The universe, then, is booby-trapped: if we venture into one of the traps or blunder upon one of the mines, then we are punished. This is sometimes called 'the wrath of God' theory. It is based on a particular reading of Scripture, especially of

the Old Testament, which positively vibrates with divine
wrath. The verse that captures it best in the New Testament is from the Letter of Paul to the Romans, chapter 1,
verse 18:

> For the wrath of God is revealed from  heaven against
> all ungodliness and wickedness of men, who by their
> wickedness suppress the truth.

The Letter as a whole is a subtle and complicated docu-
ment. Nevertheless, this text and others like it are taken
by certain thinkers and applied in a literal way. A lot of
people who would not necessarily even think of themselves as passionate believers, accept some version of the
personally rigged system: 'you sow what you reap', 'you get
what you deserve', 'if you behave irresponsibly you do not
get away with it forever', and so on. There is a lot of village
store morality around that is premised on some version of
the universe as a moral minefield.

There is another theory that is a softer version of this
and we might call it the 'impersonally rigged system'. God
is not thought of as sitting at a computer console, pushing
buttons in direct response to things done by humans on
earth, zapping them for offences, detonating his anger
against them. Instead, we are offered an automated version
of the same theory. The universe is bound by laws, it has a
causal logic, one thing leads inexorably and logically to
another. We know that fire burns, so we tell our children
not to play with it: we know that if we put our hand in the
flame, we will feel the pain and see the flesh blacken and
blister. This does not necessarily posit an angry or a
wrathful God who takes a personal interest in punishing
those who misbehave. Instead, it posits a universe of laws
and invites the wise person to discover them and live

according to them. It makes sense to behave prudently, to drive on the right side of the road, not to step off tall buildings or the law of gravity will get us, and even though there may not be maniacal laughter in the heavens as we splatter onto the pavement below, the impact will be painful enough for us.

A third answer, or, rather, attempt at explanation, is called the 'dualistic answer'. This is not so much a theory to explain the universe as it is a description of how it looks and feels to some people. There seem to be two principles contending: light and darkness, good and evil, God and what opposes God, love versus hatred, and so on. Individuals often feel these struggles within their own hearts and consciences. They are drawn to ideals of fidelity and goodness, yet something inside them lures them to self-destruction and often, indeed, to the destruction of those they love. There are theologians who believe that the God of love is, in some sense, one of the contending parties in this great battle. Far from being an aloof specta-tor of the human struggle, God is, in fact, engaged in it, dies daily, suffers eternally. There is a cross planted in God's heart. I mentioned earlier the modern feminist liturgy that captures something of this surprising and yet poetically powerful understanding of God. Instead of the conventional eucharistic prayer, 'Holy, holy, holy, Lord God of hosts', with its sense of God at the head of a mighty army, the prayer is, 'Holy, holy, holy, *vulnerable* God', sug-gesting that God is a wounded, crucified God. To many theologians and believers today, this is a troubling but appealing response to the tragic and sorrowful facts of human history.

The fourth answer is what we might call the 'deistic answer'. In deism, God does not get involved. God has made the universe and scattered it throughout space and leaves it to get on with its own business. We are on our own; we make our own meaning. The universe is a lonely and frightening place, and one of the things we can do is to try to love one another before we die. So we live by mercy and, although we may not understand plague, pestilence, and famine, we know, instinctively, that we have to oppose them, say 'no' to them. Nevertheless, we are on our own and things are just the way they are.

The fifth response is probably the most common. It is the 'agnostic response'. These are all big, interesting, but unanswerable questions. Unfortunately, we have no time to debate them, because the house is on fire, and someone is lying by the roadside who needs our help. If we stop and argue about who lit the fire or drove the car that hit the child, the house will burn to the ground and the child will die. Let us, therefore, stop talking and start acting; let us leave the answers to the questions that drill in our brains to some other time beyond time, if such a time exists.

Somewhere among those five responses most people will find themselves. My own attitude to HIV has taken a different turn. I have become persuaded that the AIDS phenomenon illuminates the gospel and is, in fact, a modern symbol of gospel love. Let me explain what I mean.

Shrove Tuesday 1993 was a busy day for me, too busy. I got home at 10.30 p.m. and realized that Lent would start in an hour and a half. Not much time left for Fat Tuesday, but I would do my best. I got out some oat cakes and cheese, opened a bottle of good red wine, and settled in front of the television. There was a programme on about a recording made in 1984 of Leonard Bernstein conducting his own musical, *West Side Story*, with José Carreras and

Kiri Te Kanawa. It made me shiver it was so good. This love story of gang rivalry in 1950s New York was full of humour and pity, love and tragedy. Everyone was clearly loving it, especially the old man himself, cigarette clamped permanently between his lips, talking about his most famous composition in his gravelly, smoky New York voice. Sitting watching it, with enough wine in me to dispose me to revelations, an angel spoke to me, a good angel, a voice from the beyond, and this is what it said: 'You know, God is not very religious'. Immediately I knew it must be true. One tends to think of God as being a bit like the Queen, having to sit through all those boring services, and here was a hint that God preferred *West Side Story*.

Behind that apparently naive claim there lies a profound theological reality. Religion is what we do with God, or, to be more precise, it is what the powerful have done with God. What the powerful always do is to control access to anything that people need or simply want. Religion, too, as an expression of power, does what power does very well: it divides and separates in order to rule. It controls access to the mystery of God by monopolies, by setting up frontiers and customs posts, and it says who is allowed through. Three classes of people are created by the religious monopolists. The most obvious is the official class, the uniformed branch that actually polices the frontiers and tells people what they can bring in and what they have to pay for. The next category are people like me with religious passports. We are allowed a certain amount of freedom of movement and partial access to the divine, but there is a big notice that always hangs above our heads: 'Have you anything to declare? You cannot get through until you have paid for those smuggled pleasures and stolen delights'. If we use the right formula, however, pay up at the frontier, we will get through, unlike people in the third category. These are the permanently excluded, by virtue of who and what they are, caught in some trap of systemic sinfulness and spiritual statelessness. Multitudes of them live out there, away off the main roads. The Bible is full of them, just as it is full of God and too full of religion. In the Bible the spiritually stateless are called outcasts and sinners, the poor, the people of the land, gentiles without the law, like the cheeky Syro-Phoenician woman we thought about earlier who told Jesus that dogs like her gobbled up the scraps of spiritual bread that fell from the tables of the elect. The Bible is full of religion and the things religion does to God, but it is also full of revolt against all official religions and it places God out there among the multitudes of the spiritually and morally stateless.

This revolutionary strand in Scripture makes three revelatory claims. The first is that all of us are on the same footing regarding God—the elder brother as well as the prodigal son. Sin and mortality define us all. William Temple expressed it well:

> Our deepest sin is always something of which we are unconscious or something of which we are proud. The sinful acts that we remember before God when we confess our sins are no more than the symptoms of our real disease. The very fact that we are able to confess them shows that they are not part of the very stuff of ourselves. But behind them all is that self-centred will, which leads us not only to prefer our way to God's, but to claim that our way, just because it is our way, must be God's way also. That is what needs to be changed; and we cannot change it.[1]

The second great claim made by this revolutionary element in Scripture is God's acceptance of us as we are. It is a recognition that not all of Scripture reflects, but it lies there disturbingly at the heart of both the New and the Old Testament, though it is probably expressed at its most powerful in Paul's Letter to the Romans, chapter 5, verse 6 and following verses:

> While we were still weak, at the right time Christ died for the ungodly. Why, one will hardly die for a righteous man—though perhaps for a good man one will dare even to die. But God shows his love for us in that while we were yet sinners Christ died for us.

This is the doctrine of the parables. We are saved by God's love for us and not by any status of our own, real or imagined.

The third claim in Scripture is that it is the outcasts who understand the meaning of this revolutionary insight into the love of God. God in Christ went to them out there, became one of them, consorted with them and told the men in uniform at heaven's passport control that the prostitutes and sinners were to get in first, thereby undermining the whole enterprise of religion.

Three claims, then, and one assumption. This is a dangerous universe and living is a risky business. God, it seems, is a risk-taker. Safety first was never a divine injunction. Those who put themselves at risk, mysteriously, put themselves close to the divine heart, and the wounded communities know the depths of the divine love in ways that the rest of us cannot even imagine. I am fumbling my way towards a statement, however tentative and unformed, that goes something like this. The AIDS epidemic and the responses to it are a very real paradigm of the gospel. We see human extremity met by unconditional love, and it is the medical profession that is the exemplar of Grace here. A friend of mine was recently tested for HIV and it became an experience of Grace. He went to see the doctor at the hospital, filled with shame and fear, and he was received by her with unconditional love. She counselled, comforted, and strengthened him. At his moment of greatest need he was met and accepted unconditionally.

In the AIDS community, however, we also encounter the bitterness and incomprehension that Christ faced. God's prophetic word always judges as well as consoles. It divided us, and so has the AIDS epidemic. The gospels are full of grumbles against the generosity of God and the extravagant love it provoked. Judas complained, because the woman who was a sinner wasted costly perfume on Jesus' feet; the labourers in the vineyard grumbled because the generous farmer paid the same wages to the latecomers as to those who had laboured all day. The same debate goes on in our own society about resource allocation, about spending money on 'people who are getting what they deserve'.

Just as the response to the AIDS epidemic has become a paradigm of the gospel, so the gospel itself must be the paradigm that the Church follows in its response to the AIDS crisis. I have recently been meditating on Jung's phrase that God's answer to Job was to become Job. This is the gospel response to the human condition and I would like to look at five consequences of it.

When I visited El Salvador during the civil war there in 1990, the people engaged in the struggle kept using a particular verb, *acompañar*: they wanted us to accompany them, to be with them in their struggle. This ought to be our response to the HIV community. We can be *with* them, present beside them; and this being with them will search our own hearts. If we let it, it will reveal to us our own prejudices. You cannot sit comfortably beside someone if you hold a moral sawn-off shotgun. We have to be beside them unconditionally.

Second, we have to name the reality, own the truth of the condition, say 'yes' to it. People with AIDS are right up against reality. They are quite good at admitting their extremity, unless society forces them to keep the knowledge secret—a terrible burden to be added to the almost unsupportable suffering. In the HIV community, there can be no denial. The running away has stopped, though there can be plenty of rage, and we must accompany them in their anger as well; we must help them to 'Rage, rage against the dying of the light'. *Their* extremity, though, should help us to name our own condition and say 'yes' to it. People with AIDS carry highly sensitive truth detectors.

The third thing to recognize is that this honest acceptance of extremity seems to be the invariable prelude to Grace. Tillich said that acceptance of our own death is the necessary prelude to revelation. It is not always that, of course, or maybe the revelation is only of the abyss, but Grace comes to us when we leave our hiding places and own who we are without condition or extenuation.

We are not only to accompany people with AIDS, however, not only to help them live with AIDS, we are inevitably, sorrowfully, overwhelmingly, going with them into their dying. The most harrowing thing about this ministry is that it calls us to accompany the young in their dying, to help them say 'yes' to the night. This is the most terrible burden that survivors bear. People working with people with AIDS, who endlessly accompany the young in their dying, are constantly wrenched by their own grief.

Their ministry puts them in what one can only describe as a state of systemic grieving. The parallel that irresistibly suggests itself to me is that other holocaust of the twentieth century, what the Jews call the *Shoa*, the destruction, the extermination of six million Jews in Germany. There is a novel that captures it for me, a novel so awful and powerful that I can turn to it only infrequently. It is *The Last of the Just*, by André Schwartz-Bart. According to the book, in every generation, in Jewish tradition, thirty-six 'just men' are born to take the burden of the world's suffering upon themselves. The book is the story of Ernie Levy, the last of the 'just men', who died at Auschwitz in 1943. At the very end of the story, Ernie is in a box car with some women and children, many of them already dead, lurching towards Auschwitz. It is Ernie's burden to console the inconsolable. The children gather round him for comfort as he cradles in his arms the emaciated corpse of a child who has just died of dysentery.

'He was my brother,' a little girl said hesitantly, anxiously, as though she had not decided what attitude it would be best to take in front of Ernie.

He sat down next to her and set her on his knees. 'He'll wake up too, in a little while, with all the others, when we reach the Kingdom of Israel. There, children can find their parents, and everybody is happy.'

'How can you tell them it's only a dream?' one of the women breathed, with hate in her voice. Rocking the child mechanically, Ernie gave way to dry sobs.

'Madame,' he said at last, 'there is no room for truth here.'

Then he stopped rocking the child, turned, and saw that the old woman's face had altered.

'Then what is there room for?' she began. And

taking a closer look at Ernie, registering all the slightest details of his face, she murmured softly. 'Then you don't believe what you're saying at all? Not at all?'

When they reach Auschwitz, Ernie leads his little flock of children into the gas chambers:

'Breathe deeply, my lambs, and quickly!'

When the layers of gas had covered everything, there was silence in the dark sky of the room for perhaps a minute, broken only by the shrill, racking coughs and the gasps of those too far gone in their agonies to offer a devotion. And first as a stream, then a cascade, then an irrepressible, majestic torrent, the poem that, through the smoke of fires and above the funeral pyres of history, the Jews—who for two thousand years never bore arms and never had either missionary empires or coloured slaves—the old love poem that the Jews traced in blood on the earth's hard crust unfurled in the gas chamber, surrounded it, dominated its dark, abysmal sneer: 'SHEMA ISRAEL ADONAI ELOHENU ADONAI EH'OTH . . . Hear O Israel, the Eternal our God, the Eternal is One.'

The voices died one by one along the unfinished poem; the dying children had aleady dug their nails into Ernie's thighs, and Golda's embrace was already weaker, her kisses were blurred, when suddenly she clung fiercely to her beloved's neck and whispered hoarsely: 'Then I'll never see you again? Never again?'

Ernie managed to spit up the needle of fire jabbing at his throat and, as the girl's body slumped against him, its eyes wide in the opaque night, he shouted against her unconscious ear, 'In a little while, *I swear it! . . .*'

The book ends:

> At times, it is true, one's heart could break in sorrow.
> But often too, preferably in the evening, I cannot help
> thinking that Ernie Levy, dead six million times, is still
> alive, somewhere, I don't know where . . . Yesterday, as I
> stood in the street trembling in despair, rooted to the
> spot, a drop of pity fell from above my face; but there
> was no breeze in the air, no cloud in the sky . . . there
> was only a presence.[2]

The only really important question in history is whether
the dream Ernie told the children is true. On the way to
Auschwitz there was no room for truth, only room for the
sustaining, impossible dream. Did Ernie believe it? Do we?

We cannot go with them into that good night, but our
ministry is not therefore ended. For us, the survivors,
there is the memorializing, the telling of the story of their
lives. AIDS has made us all remembrancers and the
Church must learn versatility in its creation of liturgies for
the unbelieving dead as well as for the grieving who are
left behind. It is possible to create liturgies of integrity
that are explicitly Godless, and liturgies we need. We need
memorials, too. Days when we help people to look back
and remember those they have loved and lost awhile.
Milestone House in Edinburgh is good at this. It has its
own annual day of remembrance and the chaplains are
good at creating liturgies that express the love as well as
the loss. Perhaps the greatest, most imaginative, most overwhelming act of remembrance is the Quilt. In 1987 a
group in San Francisco started the Names Project in
which 3- by 6-foot quilted panels, memorializing those
who have died of AIDS, are stitched into a quilt that can
now fill dozens of football pitches. It goes round the world,

reminding people of the loveliness we have lost, but it also serves as a sacrament, an outward and visible sign that this terrible thing that has come upon the human race has provoked an even more overwhelming response of love, dedication, and self-sacrifice. This is the great 'nevertheless' that the Church exists to proclaim. In spite of our own follies and pettiness, in spite of the terrible ravages of this disease and the dying of the young, *nevertheless* there is a hope against hope and it calls us to bear witness. In Camus' great novel *The Plague* (*La Peste*), a story of pestilence told by a doctor who stands up to death and says 'no', the author bears witness for those who had died of the plague and tries,

> . . . to state quite simply what we learn in times of pestilence: that there are more things to admire in men than to despise. The story could not be one of a final victory. It could only be the record of what had had to be done, and what assuredly would have to be done again by all who, while unable to be saints but refusing to bow to pestilences, strive their utmost to be healers.[3]

*That*, I suggest, should be the response of the Church to the AIDS pandemic.

# 8

## *The Cost of Caring*

There is an ancient and important philosophical distinction between grounds and causes for an action. The best way to explain the distinction is to give an example. It comes from a biography of C. S. Lewis by A. N. Wilson (Fontana 1991), and I use it simply to illustrate the point, not to agree or disagree with the view expressed by Wilson.

C. S. Lewis was converted to Christianity while he was a don at Oxford. The grounds of his conversion, the reasons he gave for it, were that he had become intellectually persuaded that there was a God; and, second, that God had come into history in the person of Jesus Christ. These were the grounds, the reasons he gave, for his conversion, but in his biography of Lewis, A. N. Wilson suggests another cause. At the time of his conversion Lewis lived with the mother of a man he had befriended in the Army during World War I, and he had promised to take care of her. Wilson believes that C. S. Lewis and Mrs Moore had a sexual relationship that was becoming increasingly difficult for Lewis to sustain. By becoming a Christian, Wison implies, Lewis would be given the perfect way out of an aspect of the relationship that had become a burden to him, and this, probably unconscious, motive was the secret cause of his conversion. The grounds, then, are the reasons we give for an action, while the causes are what actually make it happen. I suspect that most human action is a combination of rational grounds and psychological or practical causes, though each case will differ according to the circumstances. This distinction points to the ambiguity in any human undertaking. There is always a subtext, always a mixture of motives.

However, there are determinists who would claim that there is never any validity in the grounds offered for an action, except as a way of achieving intellectual respectability for something that is done for other reasons. Psychologists call this rationalizing, finding reasons or grounds for conduct actually motivated by other causes. The trouble with deterministic theories of any sort is that they are all circular and ultimately self-defeating. If everything is determined, then the doctrine that everything is determined is itself determined, so how can we evaluate it rationally? One approach to caring would be deterministic. It would claim that the emotional cost of caring is precisely what attracts people to the work in the first place. They would claim that the principle that determines all human activity is pleasure or self-satisfaction. People get into the situations they do because they want to, and what attracts people to caring is precisely the stress associated with it, the cost of it. Remove it and you remove the motivation, you take the fun out of it. Carers are stress junkies, people who need to be needed. To take the costing out of caring for them is like taking the pain out of masochism for masochists; you remove the point of the activity.

Now there probably are people of whom this could be said. If we did a personality profile of them we would discover that they derive their identity, their sense of themselves, their validation, by caring for others. They need to be needed. Wherever the need comes from, it is clearly beneficial to society, which exploits it with a vengeance. Carers of this sort collude with the exploitation. Warning them against burn-out is like telling Olympic sprinters to slow down. Burn-out is what it is all about. Some of the most effective and magnificent carers in history have been people like this. They burn with an intense white flame and consume themselves in the process. The problems presented by white-hot carers to the managers of the institutions in which they operate are complicated, but I will note only two aspects in passing: their tendency to make a universal standard out of their own psychological intensity (everyone has to do it like them); and, second, what is to be done with them in their middle age when they are, in fact, totally burned out? Middle-aged emotional veterans are a problem for any organization that is not able to pension them off handsomely, but it is not one I want to spend any time on, though it is a crucially important topic. These are the unmanageable carers, either through holiness or pathology. They streak like meteors and are gone, leaving the rest of us to handle the impossible expectations they have aroused.

What, though, about the less intense, more straightforward people in the caring professions, the people who are not stress junkies? Let me attempt a classification of stress among carers, as stress is the currency in question. I would like to suggest six elements.

The first reminds me of words they shouted at Jesus on the cross: 'He saved others. Himself he cannot save'. It has been observed frequently that professional carers are often bad at owning their own needs. In many of them there is a kind of minor Messianic complex, a need to be terrific all the time, to appear to be invulnerable. Today we distrust that complex, we recognize the importance of failure, of what they call the wounded surgeon phenomenon after T. S. Eliot's verse:

> The wounded surgeon plies the steel
> That questions the distempered part.
> Beneath the bleeding hands we feel
> The sharp compassion of the healer's art.[1]

One of the best modern therapeutic insights is that the wounded make the best healers. This is why Alcoholics Anonymous has made such a great contribution to the human sciences. There is a solidarity in weakness and shared weakness can achieve strength. Examples of the wounded healer phenomenon multiply daily, especially in the USA, where new obsessions and social and personal pathologies seem to multiply like weeds, and alongside them spring up recovery groups tailored to every type of compulsion. I had a friend in Boston who belonged to Alcoholics Anonymous, Al-Anon, Sex Addicts Anonymous, Food Bingers Anonymous, Destructive Relationships Anonymous, and one or two others. She got so addicted to recovery groups that she is now working on a group to get people off going to groups—so far they have not been able to find a free night.

A recent development in this area was provided by the Grassmarket Project in Edinburgh, which mounted a play at the Festival in 1990 and 1991 by homeless men about their lives in the lodging house and night shelter. Under the direction of Jeremy Weller, the play, *Glad*, was a sell-out and has since played in London, Paris and Berlin. During the Festival in 1991, they put on a new play, *Bad*, using boys from Polmont Borstal, and a third play called *Mad*, about the mentally ill, had a successful run during the 1992 Festival. It has been extraordinarily taxing for these young theatre producers to be permanently immersed in the violent and chaotic world of the long-term homeless or the world of the young offender and the emotionally disturbed. Only recently has some support structure been offered.

This work and much of the work done in the field of HIV is performed by untrained carers, who soon fall victim to stress. HIV is a good example of both sides of this phenomenon. Much of the cost of HIV/AIDS is borne by women ill-equipped for the task and likely to be affected personally by the virus, or through their partners, parents, siblings, children. Much emphasis is laid on the importance of such informal care by society, but it brings about enormous costs of all kinds for the carers who are also likely to be battling against a syndrome of stress from poverty, illness and poor housing already.

The problem with applying the wounded surgeon thesis to HIV/AIDS is that, essentially, we are managing an intractable condition, so the optimism, the hope of recovery, that can energize participants in other programmes is a scarcer commodity.

What all these groups show us is the importance of congruence, that is, emotional and psychological continuity, between the carer and the cared for. Unflawed healers, untroubled carers, patronize and depress us with their own apparent invulnerability. They need to learn how to acknowledge their own weaknesses and needs, if only because failure to acknowledge them will damage their sensitivity and effectiveness and create a delusionary self-image, a notoriously prevalent characteristic among the clergy.

The need to appear to be without problems is itself a source of stress. It may explain why certain brilliant surgeons who are so capable with a scalpel are notoriously blunt and insensitive in their dealings with people when they are not anaesthetized upon their tables. This is also a problem among the clergy, who are supposed to be invulnerable to all the normal human passions and doubts. Some of them think they are, of course, and they then become useless at real caring. Just owning up can be a relief, like coming out of the other closets in which we hide. Systems of pastoral care and support need to be set up for carers, though they may not be at their most effective if they are within the employing organization. This, again, is an insight that informs the best in current practice.

Statutory organizations and larger voluntary ones are often quite good at producing the kind of support systems that enable carers to share the complicated issues that face them. What, though, about carers in *small* voluntary organizations, especially in the field of HIV/AIDS? Would it not be possible for Local Authorities and larger, more established voluntary organizations, to assist these nickel and dime operations by seconding workers to them, skilled in the areas they lack? Secondment of skilled administrators and support staff would provide the type of stability that would enable the small organizations to do what they do best, which is to support and speak for individuals with HIV and their families. The cost of secondment as opposed to grant aid might be a better use of scarce resources.

Apart from the importance of acknowledging their own fears and anxieties, professional carers have to learn to live with the almost impossible tension created by the fact that they are information receivers, people who encourage others to talk and face the reality of their situation, and yet they may also have power over the lives of their informants and, indeed, may have to act on information received in favoured and confessional circumstances in a way that the individual may not be grateful for. This source of stress creates a particularly cruel dilemma for social workers, causing enormous stress and guilt, as they are less protected by traditions of absolute confidentiality than, say, the clergy.

Second, caring for others, especially the vulnerable or chronically dependent, is radically devitalizing. The heart of the problem lies in the intractability of many of the problems carers confront, leading to the treadmill effect. How do we measure success in sweeping back the tide? Enough can never be done, and recognizing that fact can afflict the carer with a desperate compulsiveness that is highly destructive. Carers have to learn the very difficult lesson of detachment, a tricky balance between proper involvement and personal survival. They have to learn that it is all right to need a break, to have had enough, to walk away—they are not responsible for the universe.

The third type of stress I call contingent stress, because it comes from being answerable to social and political structures. This is a potent source of stress in the area of children's issues. Related to it is the frontier area between caring (the primary concern and the goal carers' drives and training are aimed at) and the secondary, adversative consequences of this primary purpose. For example, in order to care for the child, the parents may have to be prosecuted. It is unlikely that the same person will always have the emotional and intellectual skills required to deal with both sides of such a case. Professional carers, whether social or hospital workers, are not well-equipped to be prosecutors. Contemporary social structures, however, increasingly do impose duties upon them for which they are rarely equipped by training or temperament, giving rise to an enormous source of stress. How it might be possible to begin to separate their function from others I do not know. I am increasingly persuaded that we expect professional carers to have a combination of attributes that is almost impossible to achieve: compassion and pragmatic discernment. The result is a psychic tug of war between their commitment to their clients and their responsibility to society.

A fourth type of stress, and one that is related to the previous type, is cognitive stress, produced by the knowledge explosion. What is real knowledge in the field of human caring? We know how cognitive systems change in all disciplines (once upon a time they kept us in bed for two weeks after an appendix operation; now they have us running round the hospital grounds within twenty-four hours). During periods of transition in knowledge systems, there is intense pressure upon practitioners, some of whom are scrupulously anxious to respond to new knowledge and feel intellectually displaced a lot of the time. Others enter recurrent phases of defensive stress, because they believed profoundly in the defeated systems and so endlessly resist the new knowledge. As no one ever blows a whistle and calls a break in the evolution of knowledge, people in the field get very battered indeed.

Perhaps the most contentious example of contemporary cognitive stress is provided by the new reproductive techniques that permit children to be conceived by donor insemination from an anonymous father, whose anonymity is protected by current legislation. Even more radical are the techniques for embryo implantation, whereby the resulting child could have two *legal* parents and two *genetic* parents. A complicating element was distractingly added by the so-called 'virgin birth' case. Modern reproductive methods make it technically possible for a woman who has never had sexual intercourse to conceive. The tabloids, inevitably, showed great interest in a recent case where a woman, without a partner, was able to give birth to a child by means of these techniques. Related to these issues is the debate concerning the moral status of foetal tissue and the ethics of sex selection. People instinctively take sides on these issues. From the point of view of the topic of this chapter, the stress comes in evaluating the rights of the infertile when they seem to counter the rights of the child.

Artificial insemination by donor (AID) is a technique that has been used for several decades and we know the effect it can have on donor offspring when they are told that they may not be given more than general details about their genetic fathers. Make full disclosure compulsory, the clinicians tell us, and the number of men prepared to donate sperm will be reduced to next to nothing. Without taking sides in this debate, it is obvious that it provides us with a good example of cognitive stress.

Another question we have to wrestle with in this field relates to the rights of the infertile themselves. How far should we go in assisting people to become pregnant? How do we decide on resource allocation issues? In a National Health Service starved of funds, on what principles do we make such decisions? Doctors, nurses, counsellors and social workers in fertility centres have found themselves heavily involved in these issues since the passing of the Human Fertilisation and Embryology Act, 1990. This is why many workers in the NHS, with no pariicularly strong political convictions, got intensely involved in the debate about reforms to the Health Service.

The fifth type of stress is political stress and it comes

in various forms. Managers of health boards and directors of finance in Local Authorities know all about budget struggles and the political in-fighting that characterizes them, but the type of political stress I really want to note comes from the social and political context of human need. Carers often see themselves as professional palliators of systemic evils who are cynically exploited by the system. For instance, those who care for homeless teenagers are intensely frustrated by a society that creates the problem in the first place and then refuses to provide adequate means to overcome it. Equally, oncologists are likely to feel conflict regarding the fact that the Government receives much of its revenue from the tax on cigarettes, whose effects confront them every day in theatre. Such carers are likely to become politically committed, however privately, and this can add its own stress in the professional context, especially in areas of political sensitivity and social volatility.

Many carers feel like refuse operatives in a throw-away society. Carers on the ragged edge of social policy, as it effects immigrants, for instance, or carers of the mentally ill as society officially moves away from institutionalization to care in the community, can experience great conflicts in their attitudes to government. There is nothing more morally destructive than being among the front-line troops in a war you do not quite believe in. It is not surprising that many nurses and social workers feel as unloved as the poor bloody infantry.

Finally, we have to note that carers, especially professional carers, are increasingly used by society as official scapegoats for intractable social problems. If we are trying to set up an AIDS facility we will become the target for vituperative abuse from the 'not in my back yard' brigade. Even more notoriously, if we are social workers engaged in the complicated phenomenon of child abuse, we are likely to become the focus of society's intense frustration at being unable to respond neatly to such an evil.

What, for instance, do we do if we are working with chronic sex offenders, when we know there is only one unit in the country that is trying to rehabilitate them? We begin to feel more like transportation officers than social workers, a ritual element in the deadly switchback of offence, arrest, imprisonment, release, then reoffence, rearrest, and so on for ever.

How do we handle the phenomenon, not of seedy and solitary sex offenders, but of networks of allegedly organized child abusers, ritualized or not? A horrendously complicated and inexact phenomenon in itself, it is made a hundred times worse by the obsessive attention of the press and broadcasting media. Their tendency is to create stories in order to be able to report them, or, by the manner of their reporting, make it almost impossible to arrive at an objective judgement.

Cumulatively, these types of stress add up to a high emotional cost. How do we handle it? I would like to end with three simple axioms. First of all, carers should prepare for stress the way riot police prepare for public abuse. They should know that stress comes with the territory. Although knowing in advance will not take the pain out of it, it might take away some of the surprise. Second, knowing that we will never eradicate it, we must learn how to manage it, through a combination of personal and group techniques. We should set up groups called 'Stressees Anonymous' in which carers can swop war stories and achieve the mysterious Grace that comes from solidarity in weakness. Finally, we must accept that stress is intrinsic to the caring professions today, and we must not get into them if we cannot cope. Instead, go off and become a Borders shepherd—or a bishop!

# 9

## El Salvador

When I lived in Boston in the early 1980s, I followed American politics, particularly foreign policy, very closely. In trying to understand the Administration's line on Central America, I remember being sceptically impressed by the intellectual toughness of Mrs Jean Kirkpatrick, the US Ambassador to the UN. One of the points she made at that time stayed with me as an interesting distinction. When asked why the US opposed oppressively left-wing regimes in Eastern Europe and Russia, yet supported oppressively right-wing regimes in Central and South America, she gave an ingenious reply. She pointed to the difference between what she called 'totalitarian' and 'authoritarian' regimes. In a totalitarian regime, everything was under the control of the government, control was total, there were no free spaces left in the community. In authoritarian regimes, however, though there was considerable oppression and government direction, there were areas of life that were relatively free, such as the freedom to practise a religion, freedom to travel abroad and the freedom to make a profit. The US role in Central America, she claimed, was to offer support to the authoritarian regimes in their own back yard, while nudging them towards democratic reforms. There was much debate in the country at the time about whether US nudging in El Salvador was strong enough to achieve genuine reforms in a country that was a very nasty example of government by the military, but there was sufficient bi-partisan support for Reagan's policy for massive US aid to El Salvador to continue.

When I took part in a Christian Aid delegation to El Salvador in January 1990, one of the things I tried to do in conversation with the people I met from the churches, co-operative organizations, foreign embassies and anyone else I spoke to, was to check out the distinction invented by Jean Kirkpatrick and find out how the evolution from authoritarianism to democracy was coming along. It was during these discussions that I heard over and over again two words that captured something of the reality of the situation in El Salvador. No sane person suggested that things in El Salvador were good for most of the people of the country. It was recognized that there was gross injustice, harsh poverty and a highly militarized environment. The only debate among sensible people was whether the situation was showing any signs of improvement, whether there was any movement towards democracy, whether there was any real political hope. One of the words that cropped up constantly was the word *espacio*, space, and it seemed to fit Mrs Kirkpatrick's distinction. Presumably, in a totalitarian society there are no spaces left to private individuals and groups that are not somehow controlled by government. If the definition of a free society is one in which achievable space for the individual is maximized in ways that do not damage the freedom of others or the well-being of society as a whole, then the people we spoke to suggested that, at various times in recent Salvadoran history, attempts had been made at reform, at opening up the situation, at creating space for political and social evolution, but that, repeatedly, these spaces had been closed up subsequently. Indeed, it was observed that one cynical interpretation of this phenomenon was that the military permitted these episodes of openness in order to get a better idea of the state of the organizations it perceived as being dangerously opposed to its own control. When the close-up came, the people who had taken advantage of the new space were quickly rounded up and imprisoned; they disappeared or they were shot. It was because of this continuing experience of failure in the evolution from authoritarianism to democracy—indeed, it was because of the perceived reversal of that process, with the movement going from authoritarianism to something more closely resembling totalitarianism—that the armed struggle had been resumed. We did not meet anyone who thought that the solution to the country's difficulties lay in the armed struggle, or that the armed struggle could be won by either side (though it was frequently noted that the FMLN would have won the war long ago if the US had not been behind the military regime in El Salvador). Nevertheless, many of the people, if not most of the people, we spoke to undoubtedly understood the frustration that had led to the uprising; and while they did not necessarily believe that force was the answer, they were realistic enough to observe that it had at least won the attention of the government and was undoubtedly influencing both the regime in El Salvador and US public opinion.

The real question for me was whether space was getting wider or narrower; and there was no doubt that, since the uprising on 11 November 1989, many of the agencies we spoke to were quite certain that their space, their freedom to operate, had been completely destroyed by the military who made repeated raids on their offices, ransacked their premises, imprisoned their workers and scared and intimidated many of their leaders who had to go into hiding or leave the country. The murder of the six Jesuits, their housekeeper and her daughter in their compound at the University in November 1989, showed that their fears were well founded.

This brings me to the second word I heard frequently, a word that has enormous force and significance in the Salvadoran theological vocabulary. It was the word *acompañar*, accompany. It is clearly a word that has an ancient Latin resonance and the word *compañero*, companion, captures this. Nevertheless, this concept of companionship has been given a new vigour and resonance by recent experiences in Central America. The people we met in the churches and aid agencies, and the theologians we spoke to, especially among the Jesuits, all used this word to express the imperative of a gospel that called them to accompany the poor, the displaced, the victims of war and to be with them in their dispossession. This insistence on accompanying the dispossessed made them intrinsically suspect to the Government. The political antonym to companionship was what the Government called *neutrality*, and it was something that the Church and the aid agencies at the grass roots level found morally impossible, even though they offered no support to the FMLN and spent much of their energy attempting to alleviate the sufferings of the people whom the guerrillas used as a shield against the army in the uprising. Because they accompanied the poor and the dispossessed who were obvious victims not only of the armed struggle but of the social and economic structures of El Salvador, they were perceived to be unsympathetic to the Government's line. This was their inescapable dilemma: in order to qualify for approval from the Government, they had to achieve a level of moral and spiritual neutrality that contradicted the very imperative that drove them to the task in the first place.

Even so, we met no one who thought that a military

solution was either feasible or desirable. All the people we met called for negotiations between the FMLN and the Government, though they realized that these would be agonizingly protracted and could probably only start outside El Salvador. We were constantly aware of a sense of the possibility of impending negotiations, and we were left in no doubt by the Deputy Head of Mission at the US Embassy, Geoff Deitrich, that the US's own internal political situation was putting pressure on the ARENA* government, hitherto perceived to be the mouthpiece of the army: first, to find the murderers of the Jesuits, and, second, to offer real evidence of a desire to achieve a negotiated settlement. All this to guarantee the success of the vote in Congress at the end of January 1990 on US military aid to El Salvador.

We also picked up a certain thread of self-interested realism within El Salvador itself. We were told that the business interests in the country were becoming depressed about their inability to attract investment or to maintain their own commercial institutions in the midst of the armed struggle, so they were moving towards the centre in a way that is historically reflected in other situations of repression where naked self-interest sometimes achieves more in a short time than decades of moral exhortation. Whether this combination of US home politics, burgeoning economic realism and war-weariness will be enough to achieve real and effective reforms in El Salvador only history will tell, though recent developments, including the ending of the war and the determination of the UN Truth Commission to bring the Death Squads to justice, are encouraging.

One of the elements that no one underestimates is the

---

*The name of the party in power.

Salvadoran army's mystical affinity with the Alamo complex, the last stand mentality. We were told that one far-right element in the army wanted the US and its aid (without which the army could not last a fortnight) off its back, so that it could go all out for the final solution. Further, even those who thought that President Christiani and the elements in the ARENA government that support him were genuine in their desire for reform were far from sanguine about the long-term future of the country.

The tragedy of the whole of Central America is that, as a single economic unit, it could probably do well, but it is now arbitrarily divided up into a series of military despotries that are staggeringly inefficient and insanely productive of human misery. Since the start of the peace process, which has been agonizingly slow, there has been some evidence of progress towards the depoliticizing of the military. Things look brighter in El Salvador than they have for a long time, but it is too soon to sing *Te Deum*.

The thing that had the most impact upon me in El Salvador was a series of moral, theological and philosophical themes that were suggested by the excruciating dilemmas that faced people there. The major theme that confronted me was the ambiguity of institutional Christianity and its often rather slippery and oblique relationship to the gospel of Christ. On the one hand, Christian institutions convey the treasure of the gospel and the radical challenge of Christ to all power; and, on the other hand, we confront the inescapable fact that the institutions that enshrine this radical challenge to power, a challenge that comes from the very heart of God, have themselves become focuses of power, aligned and allied to other powerful institutions in history. The relationship between the Catholic Church and the governments of Central America is simply a current example of an ancient and tragic theme that raises the whole problem of the acculturation of Christianity to the societies in which it is set. In situations as dramatic as the one in Central America, it is easy for outside observers to see the contrasts, but the dilution of the gospel is known in all cultures and is something that most of us, who are only moderately brave, are able to do very little about. The glory of the Church in El Salvador is that it provides not only a copy-book example of the false acculturation of Christianity, its faithless support of the mighty in their oppression of the weak, but is a vivid example of the opposite tendency. El Salvador is rich in Christians who challenge this misuse of the gospel and witness to Christ's opposition to oppression, even unto death. The Jesuit Rector of the University of South America pointed out the ancient tension between what he called the base of Christianity and its authoritarian superstructure. Of all the groups we met in El Salvador, the Jesuits were the most heroic in identifying themselves with this base in its challenge to the powers above them.

A second theme that overwhelmed me with its power in Central America was essentially a political version of this same theme of the ambiguities of institutions. It was personified in our meeting with Geoff Deitrich, the Deputy Head of Mission, within the heavily fortified American Embassy in San Salvador. He cheerfully, if somewhat cynically, set about giving us an account of US policy in its back yard in Central America. As an agent of his government's policy, he did not offer much in the way of a critique, but one could sense beneath the affable manner some of the conflict and weariness of the man of power dealing with the intractable confusions of human politics. He more or less admitted that it was unrealistic to expect the main intellectual perpetrator of the Jesuits' murder to be brought to justice, as opposed to the actual agents of the crime, though he expected (and this was before the announcement of the arrest of the soldiers accused of the slaying) that some would be arrested. They would get as high as they could, because it was expedient that some soldiers be sacrificial, so that the whole nation would not perish as a result of the withdrawal of American military aid.

As I listened to Geoff Deitrich, I had a strong sense of the weariness and frustration that Pontius Pilate must have felt confronting Jesus Christ. Politicians, after all, deal only with the possible and rarely with the ideal or the perfect. Oddly enough, the person who reminded me most of the world-weary American diplomat was a battle-scarred American priest, a Maryknoll Father, working from a bombed-out base community at Zacamil. He was only too aware of the *realpolitik* that characterizes institutional Christianity. He was a simple man, unclutterd and uncomplicated by office or power, who saw only the face of the poor, among whom he lived. He stood in his church at Zacamil—a very basic structure of breeze blocks and corrugated steel—and told us how the army had come into the empty church and shot it up. The doors and the walls were perforated with bullet holes, evidence of frenzy or frustration, and further evidence that the army was very reluctant to engage with the guerrillas and took its frustration out on targets that could not fire back, like this one, or called up the air force to bomb the *barrios*, districts that sheltered the FMLN, rather than go in and get them out one by one. Father Ron Hennessy was an old Central American hand and he had seen it all many times over. He was particularly droll on the subject of the Catholic

episcopate in Central America, with a few glowing excep-
tions, such as the martyred Oscar Romero. He was as
identified with the poor as Geoff Deitrich was with the
powerful. I do not think it was romanticism that made me
link them in my mind in a companionship of perplexity.

The final theme that hit me takes me back again to that
great word *accompany*. We were told again and again by
the groups we spoke to that they needed us to accompany
them in their struggle, to be their companions on the way;
and that delegations from abroad did help, sometimes
quite immediately and concretely, by producing a release
from prison, as was the case with Father Luís Serrano and
his companions; or more obliquely by helping to lift something of the persecution that had been visited upon them
since 11 November 1989. 'Keep coming', they said, 'don't
desert us. Accompany us in our struggle'.

What will probably remain with me longest is a series
of images of El Salvador. The most immediate image was
the one that confronted me on the day I arrived. We took
a taxi to the home of the British chargé and got lost! We
drove round the nearly deserted streets looking for the
house. All the houses in the district were protected like
Fort Knox, and when we finally arrived at the right
address and announced ourselves, the steel gates opened
and we were let in by a guard armed with a machine gun.
Whenever the British Embassy laid on transport for us it
was always in a specially fortified Land Rover, complete
with armed guards.

The second image is one I have referred to already—the
church at Zacamil, riddled with bullet holes, with the sac-
risty trashed and the vestments stolen.

The most devastating image of all, however, is of the
simple dormitory at the Pastoral Centre at the University

of Central America, where the murdered Jesuits had lived.
Father Francisco Estrada, the University Rector, took us
to the Centre and showed us the offices that had been
torched by flame-throwers, with mangled and incinerated
typewriters and copying machines. He made a special
point of showing us a photograph of Archbishop Romero,
in whose honour the Centre was built, with a single bullet
hole fired through the heart, cleanly puncturing the glass.
Murdered ten years before, they still could not stop
shooting at him.

There was much worse to come. He showed us the
simple room in which the housekeeper and her daughter
had slept, and told us how the soldiers had emptied a
magazine of bullets into each of them. Then he took us to
the corridor off which lay the Jesuits' cells, streaked in
caked blood; and outside to the garden, to the wall against
which they stood the Jesuits before riddling them with
bullets and the little lawn where afterwards they blew
their brains out. There was an Italian television crew wandering about filming the place, and the three of us stood
on the site of the slaying reciting the 'Our Father' in tears,
doubtless now a sound bite on an Italian television programme on Central America.

The next image is of the basic Christian community at
San Antonio Abad. A woman market trader, two young
mothers and a bricklayer, told us their story and shared
with us their faith, and for them Scripture was not a
tedious stranger but a strong companion. Their favourite
text was Luke chapter 4, verses 16–21.

> The spirit of the Lord is upon me because he has anoin-
> ted me to preach good news to the poor, he has sent
> me to proclaim release to the captives and recovering of

sight to the blind, to set at liberty those who are oppressed, to proclaim the acceptable year of the Lord.

Then there was the Christmas party. We were greatly helped by Father Peter McGee, a young Scottish priest working in the nunciature at San Salvador. He helped out in one of the *barrios* in his spare time and when he told his parishioners about our presence they invited us to their Christmas party. He took us to San José de la Mon-tana, a series of breathtakingly precarious corrugated iron huts, built on the side of a ravine. We were led down a narrow and winding pathway to a house where the party had been prepared. They had made ready simple food for us: we ate first, and only then did they partake. Then they sang us songs. Peter and I joined in a baritone version of *Loch Lomond*. The climax of the party was the solemn presentation of a simple jug to me, the value of which must have represented a week's wages to most of them, that is if they were employed at all. I remember thinking that if these people had the government they deserved, it would be a government of angels.

The final image is that of sitting in the guardroom at the penitentiary at Santa Ana, talking to a young prisoner, a member of the Anglican Church in San Salvador, who was anxious about himself and his wife and young children, but filled with an incredible strength and steadfastness of purpose. I told him that, like St Paul, by his very presence he was preaching to his captors. Indeed, on several occasions in San Salvador I told the poor people I met that they had re-evangelized me, made me feel once again the power and beauty and danger of the Christian gospel. The stranger in the wings had spoken yet again.

*Afterword*

# 10

## Dust and Glory

Some time ago I read again *The Life of Charles Gore* by
G. L. Prestige (William Heinemann, 1935). Gore is sometimes likened to Cardinal Newman, and they certainly
evoke from me a similar reaction: an uneasy combination
of wild attraction and secret dread. Both of them had the
spiritual aristocrat's disdain for the grubby and second-
rate. They expected and demanded a level of holiness, of
personal consecration in the life of the ordained minister
that sends shivers of retrospective anxiety down my spine.
When I think of my own half-hearted struggle after discipline and goodness, my frequent lapses, the times when I
have given up altogether and have followed the promptings
of the world, the flesh and the devil, I am filled with a
coward's gratitude that I live in a lax and tolerant era.

I have usually been careful to seek out confessors who
were known for their generous attitude to human weakness. I would have kept my distance and my secrets from
Gore and Newman; but not from Arthur Stanton, curate
of St Alban's Holborn for fifty years. Father Stanton used
to say, ' "God remembereth that we are but dust. You
can't expect dust to be always up to the mark." ' I would
have taken my dusty soul to him. He would not have
rebuked me for not being up to the mark. Yet, had I gone
to Father Stanton and heard his words of comfort and
reassurance for '. . . those sins through which I run. And
do them still, though still I do deplore . . .' I would, along

137

with relief, have received a terrible wounding, have been gripped by a searing irony. For this man who comforted me with his pitying awareness that dust could not always be up to the mark, was himself always up to the mark, despite being dust.

Like Gore and Newman, Stanton was a saint, a holy man, a being consecrated, set apart, a being surrendered, given over utterly to God. He was much cuddlier than Gore or Newman, and the common people heard him gladly when they would not have understood them, but, like them, he was a man poured out to God. I would have felt that ancient fear—the fear that the sinful always feel in the presence of holiness. I would, though, have felt long-ing, too—the longing that the sinful always feel in the presence of holiness.

This is my dilemma: I am dust and ashes, frail and wayward, a set of predetermined behavioural responses programmed by my genetic inheritance and social context, riddled with fears, beset with needs the origins of which I do not understand and whose satisfaction I cannot achieve, quintessence of dust, and unto dust I shall return. Who can expect much of that? However, there is some-thing else in me; there is an awareness that, truly, I am *not* what I am; and what I am not is what I truly am. Dust I may be, but troubled dust, dust that dreams, dust that has strange premonitions of transfiguration, of a glory in store, a destiny prepared, an inheritance that one day will be my own. How else can we account for all the fairy tales, what C. S. Lewis called the 'good dreams', that character-ize our history? All those paupers who were really princes; all those kitchen  maids who were really the king's true love; all those ugly ducklings who were majestic swans; all that glory rising from cinders and ashes. So, my life is stretched out in a painful dialectic between ashes and glory, between weakness and transfiguration. I am a riddle to myself, an exasperating enigma, 'a double-minded man, unstable in all his ways'. I am like the man in the old Jewish proverb who had two texts in his pockets, one telling him he was dust and ashes and the other that for him the whole of the world was made.

This strange duality of dust and glory that characterizes us is, I believe, a key to the understanding and interpretation of the biblical revelation. I exasperate myself. The Bible tells me that I exasperate God, too! The revelation gives us flashes, burning glimpses into God's attitude towards us. What we see there is a terrible wrestling within the divine nature as God's purpose for us, God's ambition for us, wrestles with his compassion, his knowledge of our finitude. He knows what we are made of, he remembers that we are but dust; but he longs to draw us into his glory, he offers us a share in the divine nature, and we can feel the passionate exasperation of God as he coaxes, cajoles, entices us; and then, in frustration, is stung into blazing anger by our slowness, our ignorance of the things belonging to our peace. Listen to Isaiah (chapter 5, verses 24 and 25 and chapter 9, verses 14-19):

> As the tongue of fire devours the stubble, and as dry grass sinks down in the flame, so their root will be as rottenness, and their blossom go up as dust . . .
> For all this his anger is not turned away
> And his hand is stretched out still . . .
> So the Lord cut off from Israel head and tail,
> Palm branch and reed in one day . . .
> The Lord . . . has no compassion on their fatherless and widows;

For everyone is godless and an evildoer, and every
mouth speaks folly . . .
Through the wrath of the Lord of hosts the land is
burned, and the people are like fuel for the fire . . .

Quick upon the anger, however, comes another note, this
time from Jeremiah (chapter 3, verse 12 and chapter 31,
verse 20):

Return faithless Israel, says the Lord. I will not look on
you in anger, for I am merciful, says the Lord; I will not
be angry for ever . . .
Is Ephraim my dear son? Is he my darling child? For as
often as I speak against him, I do remember him still.
Therefore my heart yearns for him; I will surely have
mercy on him, says the Lord.

This all reaches its wistful climax in Psalm 103:

The Lord is tender and compassionate,
slow to anger, most loving;
his indignation does not last for ever,
his resentment exists a short time only;
he never treats us, never punishes us,
as our guilt and sins deserve . . .
As tenderly as a father treats his children,
So the Lord treats those who fear him;
he knows what we are made of,
he remembers we are dust.

This poignant duality is never resolved in the Old
Testament, though there are hints, prefigurings of the
costly and terrible resolution in the suffering servant
passages in Isaiah. As we shall see, however, even in the
resolution God finally achieves, the duality continues, the
ambiguity abides: we are always dust called unto glory and

our lives are stretched between our beginning and our end. God's strategy respects or is bound by that ambiguity, that dialectic of dust bound for glory. I want to use it as a key, an instrument of interpretation of the glorious revelation of our salvation. We are called out of dust into a share in the divine life; our destiny is to become inheritors of the holiness of God. We are consecrated, set apart, brought out of nothing into dust and from dust we are to be brought into the kingdom of heaven. The cosmic dust, the atoms and molecules, the very particles of the universe, yea the things that are not, are called by God into his eternity.

The problem that is left unresolved in the Old Testament is *how* this frail and dreaming dust is to be consecrated, made holy, brought to its preordained perfection; how the creation is to be brought to the glory prepared for it before the foundation of the world. God's strategy for cosmic consecration, for your consecration and mine, and for the perfection of every mote of interstellar dust, is by a threefold drama of incorporation, submission, and reintegration.

### Incorporation

He partakes of our dust, takes it upon himself; in his eternal Son, God *endusts* himself. We are talking here about revelation—an unfashionable theological category at the moment, because it actually assumes that God can act towards us, make himself known, can cut through our chatter with a vision that impels silence, surrender and assent. The Church does not have a theory of the universe, a philosophy, an explanation. Our role is humbler. We have no wisdom of our own. We are entrusted with a

revelation, a showing forth of God's wisdom. Our first
task is not to explain it, but to proclaim it, to celebrate it
in baffled and adoring poetry. We sing it, and song is a
major but little-regarded test of truth. Some truths only
really exist or resonate when sung. We sing of 'The Word
of God proceeding forth, yet leaving not the Father's side'.

## Submission

God submits not only to our general condition, but to the
central reality of our state, which is death, nothingness:
we are but dust. Here I believe St Mark is the keenest witness. His Christ dies in the ashes of defeat, a burnt-out
case. He does not only taste our weakness, he absorbs it
utterly, becomes it. Dust returns to its dust.

## Reintegration

God takes this dust, this pulverized humanity, this off-
scouring, this human refuse, and brings it to the glory of
eternity. He transfigures the dust of Jesus into the eternal
humanity of Christ. The materiality of the resurrection is
crucial to its meaning. *One* handful of dust in the universe
has been consummated, restored to its divine destiny. Paul
calls the resurrection an *arrabon*, the first instalment of a
cosmic reintegration; or an *aparke*, the first fruit, the
beginning of the end for which the creation was intended.
Let me quote from Father Martelet's book, *The Risen
Christ and the Eucharistic World*:

> The Parousia will be the full emergence of the glory of a
> world much more fully incorporated in Christ by the
> resurrection than it is incorporated in human mortality
> by history, or than human history is incorporated in

the entropy of the universe. It will not be another world, in the sense of a 'duplicate' already there but invisible; rather will it be this world of ours in a completely different form, which nevertheless completes this one: it will be this world enthroned in the course of the ages, eternally, in a life without death, a being without any nil, an energy without entropy, eyes without tears, tongues without lament, hearts without sin; not a world that lies behind, but, as Teilhard says, a world which is 'ahead'. Of such a world and of its future the only herald is the risen Christ, present in a hidden manner in the folds of history, until the time comes for him there to unfold visibly his transfiguring newness.[1]

What, then, is left for us to do? Do we just wait for the return of the Christ who is present in a hidden manner in the folds of history? Yes and no. Yes and no, because, while he is glorified and has taken our dust into heaven, we are still caught in the dialectic of the dust we are and the glory that awaits us. On one level, the mystery of Christ is what Mother Julian would call a 'showing'—an exhibition, an unveiling of what is even now coming to pass. Beneath the agony and decay of the universe, God is at work restoring it, reintegrating it into its destiny. This is the mystery with which Teilhard de Chardin wrestled, and which called from him that baffling and poetic vision of a great process of cosmic transformation that, even now, is moving ineluctably towards its end.

> Step by step it irresistibly invades the universe. It is the fire that sweeps over the heath; the stroke that vibrates through the bronze.[2]

This dust is bound for glory; everything, every wounded

child and every sparrow that falls to the ground in the cold of winter is, even now, being glorified. The Church exists to point men and women to the reality of what is happening now. As the old negro spiritual puts it, 'We're on the road to glory'. There is nothing else to say in Auschwitz or in the terminal ward of the cancer hospital or by the graveside on a dark Friday afternoon. There is only that. If we felt it, if we knew it, how could the world resist us? Those who have been let in on the secret of the ages glow with the knowledge. The glory of that kingdom casts its brightness back into time and illumines the faces that look towards it: 'For it is the God who said, "Let light shine out of darkness', who has shone in our hearts to give the light of the knowledge of the glory of God in the face of Christ' (2 Cor. 4.6). That is what we see in the faces of the saints, the reflection in their eyes of the glory that has been revealed. Yes, and it can be known even now.

That glow has been caught by Catholic worship for centuries. It has irradiated Catholic lives with wit and zest, for who can be gloomy and dull when they know they are children of God, destined for the laughter and love of heaven? How I wish we could recapture that zest, the zest of those upon whom the light of the end of the ages has shone. I am not suggesting, though, that we simply stoke up our thuribles, stand in front of our golden reredoses, lock the doors against the cries and laughter of those outside, and take a glory trip.

> . . . under the Travers baroque, in a limewashed
>    whiteness,
> The fiddle-back vestments a-glitter with morning rays,
> Our Lady's image, in multiple-candled brightness,
> The bells and banners—those were the waking days
> When Faith was taught and fanned to a golden blaze.[3]

Even so, I am not going to knock that kind of thing. Like everyone else, from Sir John Betjeman to Barbra Streisand, I believe that a bit of nostalgia for the way we were does not do much harm. The difficulty is always the same: how to keep the glory-vision of the end-time aflame *and* get on with our work in the world now. Let me quote from the Constitution on the Church of Vatican II:

> The final age of the world has already come upon us. The renovation of the world has already been irrevocably decreed and in this age is already anticipated in some real way. For even now on this earth the Church is marked with a genuine though imperfect holiness. However, until there is a new heaven and a new earth where justice dwells, the pilgrim Church in her sacraments and institutions, which pertain to this present time, takes on the appearance of this passing world. She herself dwells among creatures who groan and travail in pain until now and await the revelation of the sons of God.[4]

It seems to me that the Church's life in the world as it wrestles with problems of its own institutional life, the challenge of evangelism, and the complicated ethical issues that face it, is best interpreted in the light of the often baffling ambiguity of its own status as consecrated dust. It is always stretched between these two poles, and the duality is seen sometimes within the same person, more often between different types. Our Lord and St Paul bore the tension within themselves, but those who have followed them have tended to draw out one meaning and systematize it: so, you get justification by faith alone, and its pathological concomitant, antinomianism; or you get the call to holiness, and its pathological concomitant,

puritanism. I want to describe some aspects of this permanent tension in the life of the Church under two, often
apparently contradictory, headings: the glory strategy and
the dust factor.


## The glory strategy

There are always those, whether raised up by God or
impelled by some form of self-righteousness, who call the
Church or the world to an absolute standard. In politics
they are usually utopians, in morals they are usually puritans, in Church discipline they are usually rigorists. As a
result, they are always in a more or less adversarial state
towards their fellows. They are consumed with an end-
vision. Karl Barth said that ethics cannot exist without
millenarianism, however small the dose, and he was right.
However, the glory strategist, by definition, does not
believe in *small* doses of holiness, or justice; the glory
strategist wants it in its completeness.

Now, I am not a glory strategist, so I am bound not to
be entirely fair to them. This is partly because they make
me feel guilty, and partly because I believe their perfec-
tionism often has tragic results. In politics, for instance, I
believe that attempts to create the new heaven on earth
usually only lead to the old hell. In morals, I am closer to
them in theory, because, like a lot of people, I believe
their emphasis needs reasserting in the situation of moral
relativism that characterizes today's culture. Even so, they
make me feel uneasy. In Church discipline, I am frankly
confused and do not quite know which way to turn. The
strange thing is that we rarely get a complete glory strategist, that is, one upholding such a philosophy in politics,
private morals *and* Church discipline. For example, political

utopians in Anglican circles are often also ecclesiastical disciplinarians, but, in my experience, they are rarely puritans.

## The dust factor

I am more at home with the dust factor, though I am conscious that this might be just an easy option. I suspect that most pastors, most priests, tend to be in this corner; that is why they make lousy prophets and often end up stoning those sent to them.

Like Arthur Stanton, pastors rarely expect dust to be up to the mark, so they are suspicious of political programmes that presuppose the emergence of a perfection that their experience has led them never to expect. In morals they are not very good at seeing the wood because they know, love, and lament over so many of the trees. For instance, homosexuality is not a moral *issue* for them—it is Jim and Harry, their confusion, frailty, and search for love. The remarriage of the divorced is not an ecclesiastical issue for them—it is a succession of people they know, often stunned by failure and desperate to redeem it in a new future. Maybe even the ordination of women is not an issue so much as a person, quiet, pacific, unaggressively but surely aware of her vocation. See what perils pastors are in by virtue of their close identification with those they serve? That is why they are rarely prophetic.

It goes even deeper than that, though, because they often know themselves to be broken men, men with nothing to boast about, no holiness to point to. Graham Greene is the great celebrant of the whisky priest, the promiscuous priest. Their broken hearts are well attested. Who, though, is to uncover the pain of the comfy priest,

the quiet and worldly priest, with his middle-class yearn-
ings, contained in the same breast as the knowledge of the
glory of God in the face of Jesus Christ? They save others;
themselves they cannot save.

So, we are caught in a painful tension between a searing,
angry, judging ethics of glory and holiness, filled with the
true vision of what ought to be; and a wistful, pitiful,
pragmatic ethics of dust, rendered hesitant by an overwhelming awareness of what is. Glory and ashes; the end
and the beginning; then and now. How can we resolve it,
live with it, be one Church, one person, when this tension
tears us apart? Well, remember, this is where we came in.

Does this not describe the heart of God, consumed
with a terrible and eternal ambition for us, and yet made
weak and tender by his loving awareness of our nothingness? How can we escape what breaks his heart? Remember,
too, the resolution. It was in Jesus. In him, ashes pertained
to glory; in him, anger and pity kissed each other; in him,
holiness and compassion became one; in him, prophet
and priest at last joined hands. Only in him and in his
way are these tensions resolved. Only as we each grow
into him can we grow towards each other.

However, I have a fear that this might not happen. I
have a fear lest these tensions within the Church will
simply tear it apart because we will each go our own way,
not his; and there is no human agent that can bring all
this together. I fear lest we start playing church politics,
adopting pressure-group tactics, start throwing down
gauntlets. Only the press and the despisers of the Church
will profit from that. That cannot be our way. Catholic
renewal must be growth in the heart and likeness of Jesus
or it will be death, not life. There is a historical precedent

for this. The thing that killed off the evangelical revival of the nineteenth century was the negative campaign it mounted against those it opposed in the Catholic movement within the Church of England. It created an uproar, a hullabaloo, as it opposed trends and tendencies it deplored. It was successful, too, for a time; but only in stopping something, not in doing anything. Unfortunately, that is how it came over to people, as a movement that was not *for* anything, but as a movement that was simply *against* something. Negative movements, like negative theology, do not capture the hearts and minds of good men and women, only those of the sick-minded, the marginal, the insecure. That could, but must not happen to Catholic Renewal. We must not become a fanatical, self-righteous rump, a sort of ecclesiastical National Front. We will only avoid this, however, if we will turn to him who bears all these tensions still upon his heart. Let this movement be a great turning towards him.

Father Stanton once told a group of ordinands, 'When you're priests, tell your people to love the Lord Jesus. Don't tell them to be C. of E. Tell them to love the Lord Jesus'. I can think of nothing better as a motive and motto for Catholic Renewal in the Anglican Church: go and tell them to love the Lord Jesus.

---

The words I spoke at Loughborough in 1978, proved to be tragically predictive. Increasingly, opposition to the ordination of women to the priesthood became the litmus test of catholicity. Since the vote in the General Synod of the Church of England on 11 November 1992, there are members of the Catholic tradition in Anglicanism who now assert that the act of ordaining the first woman in the

Church of England will, as it were, decatholicize the Church of their birth. I do not wise to rehearse here things I have written elsewhere on this issue, particularly in *Who Needs Feminism?* (SPCK 1991), but I recall this episode here, because it is the most powerful and tragic recent example of a tendency in Christianity to which I have referred several times in this book—the tendency to see Christianity not as a dynamic movement in history, but as a protectionist sect, chosen to guard and watch over a fixed and static deposit of truth. The logic of such an interpretation of Christian tradition is sectarian rather than Catholic, static rather than dynamic, defensive rather than bold.

There are many examples of religious defensiveness of this sort in today's turbulent world and it is no accident that the fundamentalist mind is angrily at work in all faith systems, including Islam and Hinduism. Negative movements can have enormous power in any tradition for a time because they appeal to our anxieties and fears, but they do not endure. The text for all these struggles is firmly embedded in one of the earliest documents of the Christian Church, where Gamaliel warned the Sanhedrin not to persecute the Christan movement, because if it was not of God it would not succeed and if it was of God it was futile to oppose it. Zealous reactionaries never learn this wisdom. Invariably, something that was written in *Vanity Fair* about a noted Anglo-Catholic priest is applicable to such people, that they are 'endowed less with a great power of will than with an enormous power of won't'. Passionate conservatives always refuse to accept the organic nature of the Church in history. They resist all development and change, usually unintelligently, and by their persecution of the new idea or practice breed the very sympathy for it that is so contrary to their own intentions. We are witnessing one of these episodes in the Anglican Church today. The supreme irony is that, of all the traditions in Anglicanism, the Catholic tradition ought to have learned this lesson best, having won its case against the persecution mounted against it by the Church Association at the close of the nineteenth century. This great movement that changed world Anglicanism for ever and revolutionized its liturgy is now acting like the Church Association in lace cottas. It is the great negative movement today, opposing developments in the Church's ministry that would make it inclusive of the whole human race rather than the male half of it.

The final paradox is the deeply Protestant nature of Anglo-Catholicism. The word 'Protestant' can be used in many ways. I am using it here in its sense of protest against the abuses of authority. The Anglo-Catholic fathers were deeply Protestant in their refusal to conform to the authority set over them, both in the Church and the State. They always appealed, in a very Protestant way, to a higher authority, that of primitive Catholic Christianity. This was the appeal made by the great Protestant reformers as well. It was the very Protestantism of the Anglican Church that gave Catholics the space and the freedom to make their protests and to win their cause. The intellectual tragedy of Anglo-Catholicism is that it has never acknowledged that it was the very element in Anglicanism it most passionately repudiated that guaranteed its own right to protest. It is the critical, evolving, prophetic element in Christianity that makes it a living faith for today.

Various versions of Christianity are in contention today and the struggle will become increasingly passionate as we move towards the second millennium. I quoted earlier Franklin Roosevelt and cited him as an example of a person with a confident attitude towards the future. It is more than human optimism that guarantees our confidence, it is the knowledge that our God is God of the future as well as the past and will be found in what we do not yet know as well as in what we do. We have nothing to fear except fear itself.

# References

## Chapter 1

1 Alfred, Lord Tennyson, 'The Princess'.
2 Miguel de Unamuno, tr. J. E. C. Flitch, *Tragic Sense of Life*. Dover 1976.

## Chapter 2

1 Kathleen Raine, *On a Deserted Shore* (Poem 95). Dolmen Press: Dublin 1973.
2 'Look back. . . and etc.' – can't trace author.
3 Isaiah Berlin, *Oxford Book of Essays*. OUP 1991, p. 557.
4 Louis MacNeice, *Collected Poems*. Faber & Faber 1979, p. 195.

## Chapter 3

1 Answer on being asked her opinion of Christ's presence in the Sacrament. S. Clarke, *Marrow of Ecclesiastical History* (pt ii, Life of Queen Elizabeth, ed. 1675).

## Chapter 4

1 Translation of Boethius by Helen Waddell in *Mediaeval Latin Lyrics*. Constable 1975, p. 49.

## Chapter 5

1 Peter Henessy, *Never Again: Britain 1945–51*. Vintage 1993.

2 Quoted in full in *RSA Journal* (Vol. CXL, No. 5432, August/September 1992).
3 Ibid.

## Chapter 6

1 Pontifical Commission, *What Have You Done to Your Homeless Brothers?: Church and the Housing Problem.* Veritas 1988.
2 Ibid.

## Chapter 7

1 William Temple, extract from 'Holy Week', on BBC. 1942.
2 André Schwarz-Bart, *The Last of the Just.* Penguin 1960.
3 Albert Camus, chapters 2, 3 and 4, *The Plague.* Penguin 1989.

## Chapter 8

1 T. S. Eliot, 'East Coker', published in *Collected Poems.* Harcourt, Brace & Co. 1952.

## Chapter 10

1 S. Martelet, *The Risen Christ and the Eucharistic World.* Collins 1976.
2 Teilhard de Chardin, *The Divine Milieu*, pp. 102–4 cited in Martelet, op. cit..
3 Sir John Betjeman, *High and Low.* John Murray 1966.
4 Constitution on the Church of the Second Vatican Council No. 48 Catholic Truth Society.